LOST BAB BALLADS

LOST BAB BALLADS

BY

W. S. GILBERT

Collected Edited and Illustrated by
TOWNLEY SEARLE

LONDON & NEW YORK

G. P. PUTNAM'S SONS LTD

First Published September, 1932

*Of this First Edition a limited number of copies are issued
with hand-coloured illustrations*

Reprinted October, 1932

PRINTED IN GREAT BRITAIN BY
CHARLES WHITTINGHAM AND GRIGGS (PRINTERS), LTD.
CHISWICK PRESS, BRUNSWICK PARK ROAD, N.11.

INTRODUCTION

THESE " Lost " or " Uncollected " " Bab Ballads," originally appeared in the pages of *Fun, Punch, Hood's Annual, The Comic News* and similar publications. They are now reprinted by kind permission of Lady Gilbert, and the reason they were not collected during the author's lifetime was because, in the words of Sir William Gilbert, he thought " the public have enough already—the book is already too big." Posterity, however, has seen fit to disagree with the author and has said quite plainly that we cannot have too much of " The Bab Ballads."

These uncollected Ballads come before the present generation as an entirely new book, for few except the ardent Gilbertian " Collector " will have taken the time and trouble to seek out these fugitive writings from journals, some of which are to-day extremely difficult to obtain.

It is many years since the first of the " Bab Ballads " appeared in the pages of *Fun*, but we can believe that there were then among its readers some few who, picking up their favourite sixpenny weekly on the first day of June, 1867, were able to appraise at something like its true literary value the humorous verse therein contained.

At this time there were two humorous weeklies vieing for popular favour. Once, Gilbert enquired of the editor of the older journal, as to whether *Punch* EVER received any good jokes, and upon receiving a dignified reply to the effect that the premier humorous weekly most certainly received many excellent jokes, Gilbert asked, " Why don't you print some of them? " It is with little surprise therefore that we

Introduction

learn that *Punch* " declined with thanks " Gilbert's first contribution of a " Bab Ballad," and that thereafter he and the editor occasionally belaboured each other in print or otherwise.

Sir W. S. Gilbert was born on 18th November 1836, before Queen Victoria came to the throne, and he thus lived in four reigns. Educated partly at Boulogne, he took his degree at the London University in 1857, and it was in that year that he made what he called his " very first plunge." From his first translation of the " laughing song " in " Manon Lescaut," he continued as a maker of merriment with the " Bab Ballads," the first of which appeared in the humorous journal *Fun* in 1861.

" The Yarn of the Nancy Bell," declined by *Punch*, was first printed in *Fun* in 1866 and created such a furore that the publishers were inundated with requests for separate publication with appropriate music. The ballad soon became the favourite piece with amateur reciters, and Alfred Plumpton, who afterwards became musical director at the Palace Theatre, obliged with a musical setting.

Gilbert's association with Sir Arthur Sullivan began in 1871, when he developed the vein of humour indicated in the " Bab Ballads."

In my recent book, *Sir W. S. Gilbert: A Topsy-Turvy Adventure*, I was able to trace some of the author's known and most successful work to such sources as verses for popular magazines, etc. The original germ of " Trial by Jury " was written as a " fill-up " for a page of *Fun*, and was afterwards expanded into a full page with four illustrations, before it was finally produced as one of the most successful comic operas. Again, " An Old Score " was first printed in what would to-day be called " scenario " form in the same journal.

In this present collection, it will be seen that there are

Introduction

two or three Ballads written round " Curates," and it was this " Curate business " that upset Lewis Carroll, who could never forget that he was the Rev. Mr. Dodgson.

The author of *Alice in Wonderland* was Gilbert's most severe critic, and wrote in *The Theatre Magazine* in 1888:—

" Mr. Gilbert seems to have a craze for making bishops and clergymen contemptible. Yet are they behind other professions in such things as earnestness, and hard work, and devotion of life to the call of duty? That clever song, ' The Pale Young Curate,' with its charming music, is to me simply painful. I seem to see him as he goes home at night, pale and worn with the day's work, perhaps sick with the pestilent atmosphere of a noisome garret where, at the risk of his life, he has been comforting a dying man —and is your sense of humour, my reader, so keen that you can laugh at that man? Then at least be consistent. Laugh also at that pale young doctor, whom you have summoned in such hot haste to your own dying child; ay, and laugh also at that pale young soldier, as he sinks on the trampled battlefield, and reddens the dust with his life-blood for the honour of Old England! "

Again, after witnessing a performance of " H.M.S. Pinafore," Lewis Carroll wrote:—

" One passage was to me sad beyond words. It occurs when the captain utters the oath ' Damn me! ' He said, ' Damn me! ' I cannot find words to convey to the reader the pain I felt in seeing dear children taught to utter such words to amuse ears grown callous to their ghastly meaning. Put the two ideas side by side Hell (no matter whether you believe in it or not; millions do), and those pure young lips thus sporting with its horrors— and then find what fun in it you can! How Mr. Gilbert could have stooped to write, or Sir Arthur Sullivan could have prostituted his noble art to set to music, such vile trash, it passes my skill to understand."

It was precisely this sort of exaggerated piety that Gilbert rejoiced in ridiculing, and his " vile trash " is to-day as popular as are the works of his reverend critic.

They both thrived in the joyous days of the 'seventies, when the Franco-German War had handed over to England the profitable commerce of the world. Everyone had money and the nation wanted to laugh. The " topsy-turvydom " of Gilbert's humour came along at a time when the French comic opera was on the wane, and as Gilbert's humour was something entirely new and withal entirely English, it was very acceptable.

Gilbert was poet, sentimentalist, and humorist, and the perfection of his rhythms and metres indicated the delicate mind that could never be guilty of an error of taste.

Colonels and Curates, Snobs and Swells, Knights and Ladies, " Bandoline " Players and Babies, Wicked Barons and Sentimental Serfs—all the old favourites are here set out for your delight.

TOWNLEY SEARLE.

London, *September* 1932.

CONTENTS

Contents

LOST BAB BALLADS

THE BARON KLOPFZETTERHEIM;

OR,

THE BEAUTIFUL BERTHA AND THE
BIG BAD BROTHERS OF BONN

NEAR the town of St. Goar,
  On the bleak Rhenish shore,
Dwelt a terrible baron—a certain
  KLOPFZETTERHEIM.
  I've not got it pat,
  But it sounded like that,
Though whether it's properly
    spelt to the letter, I'm
  Not at all sure; I
  Confess for this story
To memory (second-rate) only a debtor I'm.
  Indulgence I claim,

The Baron Klopfzetterheim

It's a high-sounding name,
And a name, too, to which one
    can easily set a rhyme.

  A growling and gruff'un,
  A ruthless and rough'un,
A tyrant, a Tartar, a toothless and tough'un;
His skull was as bald as the palm of my hand,
And surrounding its base was a silvery band
Of curly grey hair, and he brushed it well up
  From ear round to ear,
  So it looked, from the rear,
Like a very smooth egg in a very white cup.
  He'd bricks, and he'd mortar;
  He'd wood, and he'd water;
Sheep, oxen and poultry, calves, pigs and—a daughter;
Whom, though generally such points rather lax on, he
Swore was the loveliest woman in Saxony.

  The baron was wealthy, but horribly stealthy;
  He'd jewels from Ingy, but still he was stingy;
  Though rich from a babby, unbearably shabby;
  Though steeped to his eyes, sir, in wealth, yet a miser;
From boyhood a dunce, always trying to shirk " hic, hoc,
Hæc," he was stupid and proud as a turkey-cock.
  Stealthy and stingy and shabby and miserly,
  Every morning his wont was to rise early;
  Search out each inch of his rocky dominions,
  Count all the eggs and the apples and iniuns,
  Listen at keyholes for candid opinions
  Propounded by uncomplimentary minions,
    In syllables bated,
    For so was he hated
By all his dependents, for reasons just stated.

The Baron Klopfzetterheim

 Superior far,
 To her horrid papa,
Was BERTHA. The daughters of barons oft are.
 Her hair was fair,
 And a flaxen rare;
In the fine land called Rhineland the best, I declare;
Its charms, in a single comparison summing,
It looked like a " nimbus," but far more becoming;
Besides, you could brush it, and alter the sit of it,
Play with its folds (did decorum permit of it),
Tickle your cheek with a stray ray or so;
Now you can't do all that with a " nimbus," you know.
Flaxen, I said—I recant—not a bit of it;
 A glorified hue
 (You find it on few),
Gold mingled with brown—now I'm sadly put to
 For an elegant noun
 (It must be gold and brown)
 To which I can liken this natural crown;
But commonplace thoughts prove effectual stoppers,
And I can't think of any but sovereigns and coppers.

In length it was ample, as you may suppose,
 For when BERTHA so fair
 Let down her back hair,
 It rippled away till it reached to her toes.
She'd have made (had necessity ventured to drive her)
 A really respectable Lady Godiva.
It was long, it was silky, and wavy, and mellow,
And about as much " flaxen " as sunbeams are yellow.

 Then her eyes!
 Their size!
 Their glorious blue!

The Baron Klopfzetterheim

I'm sure it's a hue!
That was solely invented our trials to leaven—
You'll find it alone in girls' eyes and in heaven!
When nobody hailed them
She quietly veiled them,
Humanely declining
To send you, by needlessly flashing their light at you,
Hopelessly pining;
But when you addressed her she always looked right at you—
Right in your face,
With a maidenly grace,
That spoke to the truth and sincerity there,
And misconstrue that innocent gaze if you dare!

Now the Baron's old seneschal
Finding the Rhenish all
Swallowed, he hied
For some more to the marchand de vin, who replied,
" Friend, never of Rhenish the worth of a penny shall
E'er again aid in his Lordship's digestion,
Unless he first pays down the penny in question.
The Baron must think me as green as an olive! Hence he
Ne'er will get more without cash down, at all events he
Couldn't suppose I would act with such folly ven see "
(Opening his books
With disheartening looks),
" I am tottering just on the brink of insolvency "
So the seneschal thought
It was time to report
To his master the crisis to which he was brought.

'Tis time now, I grieve, to my story to weave two who love
to deceive, and to plunder and thieve,

4

The Baron Klopfzetterheim

And this, by your leave, I'll attempt to achieve in a style,
    I believe, known as recitative.

A neighbouring Pfalzgraf had three sons, and he in armour
    glistened 'em;
Rupert, Carl and Otto, as their noble father christened 'em.
In Christendom than Otto you would hardly find a finer
    knight;
He set the women's hearts a-fire, which blazed away like
    pine a-light.
To gain him, all the German mothers tried the worst
    rascalities,
For he possessed the greatest of the German principalities;
    In fact, it brought him clear
    THREE HUNDRED POUNDS A YEAR—
Enough, we know, to sanction matrimonial formalities.

Now as Rupert was eldest, and Carl was the second,
And Otto the youngest, I'll swear you'll have reckoned
That Rupert and Carl were, to say the least, quite on
    A par, as to evil
    With Robert, the Devil,
  And Otto a second edition of Crichton,
    In legends we know
    That it always is so:
The eldest sons, villains unheard of are thought to be;
The youngest, however, is just what he ought to be.
  Otto was graceful, and slender, and tall,
  While Rupert and Carl were as round as a ball.
  Otto was handsome and neat as a pin,
  While Rupert and Carl were as ugly as sin.

Now Rupert and Otto and Carl one day,
As home from hunting they made their way,

5

The Baron Klopfzetterheim

They entered the wine-merchant's cabaret;
Two brandies and water were brought on a tray
    (For excellent Otto
    Knew he ought not to
Drink anything stronger than curds and whey);
Then listened awhile to the gossiping host,
    Who merrily told
    Of the miserly old
Baron Klopfzetterheim, rolling in gold—
    Of his recent endeavour
    To get wine, and never
Pay nobody not even nothing whatever;
    Telling them further,
    How nowhere on earth a
More opposite creature existed than Bertha
    (His amiable daughter),
    How lovely all thought her,
And how he drove off all the nobles who sought her.

Now Otto and Carl were cunning and bold,
    And resolved to get hold
    Of the jewels and gold,
In which it was said that Klopfzetterheim rolled.
But Otto was cast in a different mould,
And couldn't help thinking of what he was told
Of the beautiful Bertha, shut up by her old
    Unpopular father
    (Proprietor, rather);
    So high-minded Otto
    Remarked (voce sotto),
" These matters a pretty condition have got to;
    Quite free from this fetter I'm
    Resolved for to set her—I'm
Dashed if I'll suffer the Lord of Klopfzetterheim

The Baron Klopfzetterheim

    Thus to imprison
    So lovely a miss, on
The highly illogical plea that she's his'n."

Now the two elder brothers resolved to confide
In the landlord, and promised with him to divide
    The results, if he'd let them bide inside
    Two barrels, and so to the castle ride,
      To the Baron's old Rhenish hall,
    As though 'twere the liquor so rudely denied
      To the Baron's old seneschal.
So each of these worthies was packed in a barrel,
But what with their size and their flowing apparel,
    'Twas such a tight fit,
    That they couldn't e'en sit,
  Turn, stoop down, or change their position a bit;
    Only waiting to ask
    For a lantern and mask,
They ordered the landlord to " head in the cask."

Good Otto, not knowing
What matters were doing,
Or thinking in which way the wind it was blowing,
Paid what was owing
For what they'd been stowing
Away in their waistcoats—then thought about going,
When he saw at the door
A wine cart with four
Strong horses attached, and of Rhenish a store;
And on asking the host,
How now lay the coast,
Was astonished to find
That he'd quite changed his mind,

And was going to send both the wine and the car on
To his lordship and eminent highness the baron.

Now being a brave and intelligent unit, he
Thought he could see a first-rate opportunity
Of seeing Miss Bertha with perfect impunity.
    It was not to be lost;
    So he said to the host,
" If you'll dress me like one of your active young draymen
(I'm sure I shall look like a chick of the same hen),
I'll pay you right nobly, as I always pay men."
The host, though the most irreligious of laymen,
Responded to this with a clerical " Amen ";
    And quickly equipped him,
    Be-frocked and be-whipped him,
  And Otto, on his part, unsparingly tipped him,
    Then started away,
    With the wine in the dray,
  Completely disguised in his drayman's array.
    But pondering arter
    The baron's fair darter,
He failed to remember his rôle as a carter,
And nearly created the dickens's own " to do,"

    For he knocked with a bang,
    And he noisily rang
As gentlemen visitors only are wont to do;
    Although I may tell
    You, he knew very well
That a modest appeal at the area bell
Would, in his new line of life, better have fitted him,
As the flunkeys with justice remarked, who admitted him—
Adding some curses which nearly concerned his eyes;
But Otto, the mild, from these wicked men turned his eyes,

The Baron Klopfzetterheim

Contented with gently consigning to Bath them as
Hurled at his head those unholy anathemas.

    The Baron Klopfzetterheim—
    Deeply in debt, or I'm
Greatly deceived (how these German names fetter rhyme!)—
    Opened his eyes
    With excessive surprise,
  As he saw the two casks of respectable size
With Rhenish replete; and he opened them wider
When Otto suggested, by way of a rider,
His master's (the wine merchant's) deepest regret
(Expressed in a note for his lordship's perusal)
    That his foreman had let
    A ridiculous debt
Occasion the baron so coarse a refusal;
But as it was done without even his knowledge, he
Trusted the baron would take his apology
    In the way it was meant,
    For the wine he'd have sent
In a second (the shortest space known in horology).

The baron, delighted, was easily pacified,
    For when Rhenish fails
    He falls back upon ales,
And gets—p'raps not tipsy, but just rather Bass-ified
(The stages of drink are not easily classified—
I'm speaking or writing about it, just *as* if I'd
Studied a failing, which horrid and fell I call);
In short, he was just in a humour angelical.
So he ordered Sir Otto to take down each cask
To the cellar, and told off Miss B. to the task
    Of watching it's storing
    In wine cellar, roaring

9

The Baron Klopfzetterheim

And shaking his stick at poor Otto (a penny thing);
He told her to watch lest he pocketed anything.

    Otto goes to the cellar
    With Bertha la bella
(Who, like a good girl, always does what you tell her),
Assisted by many a half-starved retainer;
    But lost to his duty
    In Bertha's great beauty
(Many men have been dazzled by many a plainer),
    He made a mistake that he didn't observe—he
Placed each of the casks on the ground topsyturvy,
And the horrible consequence was, that instead
Of his feet, his two brothers stood each on his head!

    Now figurez vous
    The terrible stew
Of two young noblemen (stout ones, too),
Each in a cask, which a clumsy crew
Had topsy-turvy placed, in lieu
Of setting it down as they ought to do!
Of course these people none of them knew
Of the couple of nice young gentlemen, who
Were turning a most unusual hue,
From scarlet and purple to indigo blue,
As the blood to their head in a cataract flew;
Who'd have raised in a roaring hullaballoo,
But that they feared to furnish a clue
To their hiding-place, for they thought on a few
Of the terrible things that would then fall due.
So they cursed away at each clumsy boor,
As their chances of life grew fewer,
They swore that gold should never allure
Their innocent minds to thoughts impure;

10

The Baron Klopfzetterheim

But in spite of these good resolves, these poor
Young men grew bluer, and bluer, and bluer.

It's always an awkward thing, popping the question—
Refusals agree with few people's digestion;
So nine out of ten men are dreadfully slow about it—
Their minds are unsettled and change to and fro about it,
Because they don't know how young people should go about
    it;
    They hesitate so about it,
    So frightened, I trow, about it;
They deserve to get married, and that's all I know about it.

    Otto well knew
    That the right thing to do
Was to say what he meant, and in syllables few.
    So he ventured to say,
    In his tenderest way,
    " The man now before you
    Lives but to adore you."
(With all that he said I'm not going to bore you;
Not that I'm anxious to make any myth of it,
But I think you'll be satisfied, quite, with the pith of it;
He talked as talk Wilkinson, Johnson, or Smith of it.)
    Then his right hand he placed
    Round her delicate waist,
As well as he was in the cellar pitch-dark able.   He
Wound up by adding, " I love you re-mark-able-y; "
And when Bertha indignantly answered him, " What, man
An offer—he! ha!—from the family potman!
My father your hide with his cudgel shall flay, man,
And teach you respect, you impertinent drayman;
In a moment your insolent manners he'll cure! "
" I'm no more a drayman," says Otto, " than you're—

The Baron Klopfzetterheim

A proof I'll afford you of this satisfactory; "
And though an extremely indifferent actor, he
Took from his waistcoat a big parchment roll, and
Proceeded to go through " The fair land of Poland,"
And handed the deed at the ballad's conclusion
To Bertha, who stood overwhelmed with confusion.

    She read the recitals
    Of honours and titles,
From the opening words of the deed—" THIS INDENTURE,"
To " Witness whereof," with the air of a bencher
(That she understood nothing, my fortune I'll stake on it).
Then remarking she'd no requisitions to make on it,
With appropriate action to Otto returned it,
And let him shake hands; and I think he had earned it.

    Oh, careful papa!
    Oh, prudent mamma!
Oh, uncle! oh, brother! which ever you are,
    Whose well-lighted halls
    See parties and balls,
Whose daughters go out and pay stiff morning calls,
    And who think this proceeding,
    Of which you've been reading,
Not quite in accordance with ladylike breeding—
Remember her father, detestably mean,
Whose servant for fifteen long years she had been—
Cooking poor dinners and scrubbing floors clean,
And that Otto was always considered, I ween,
The handsomest noble that ever was seen.

Otto told her, the reason he wore a disguise,
Was to bask unrestrained in the light of her eyes.

The Baron Klopfzetterheim

Then he made a neat speech about God of Love's dart,
And offered his house, and his hands, and his heart
(And whenever he mentioned that organ, he thumped at it);
She didn't reject it—I may say, she jumped at it;
And Otto had such a peculiar way with him,
She agreed to elope from the castle that day with him,
If he could but discover (she'd many a doubt of it)
Some way by which she might get unobserved out of it.
But Otto's good luck set him in the right track again;
There were two empty casks, he remarked, to go back again,
And he thought that Miss Bertha could nicely arrange
(With judicious curtailing of under apparel),
To cram herself comfortably in a barrel.
So she ran upstairs once just to pack up a change;
This done to her own satisfaction, she bade an
Undoubtedly faithful (though saucy) handmaiden
    Instanter prepare,
    By smoothing her hair
And " cleaning " herself (which a washing soap meant—
It's not a nice phrase), for a sudden elopement.

Then Bertha and Gretchen descended to Otto
(Who was wondering where in the world they had got to)
And at first he demurred, when he heard she preferred
To take with her a third, and he thought it absurd
That she'd not go alone in her Otto's society,
And all for the purpose of playing propriety.

    With squeezing and crushing,
    And crowding and pushing,
And crying and flushing, and chuckling and blushing,
They entered the casks (each of which held a cushing).
    Miss B. began brushing
    The tears that were gushing,

The Baron Klopfzetterheim

And Otto, outside, enjoined silence by " hush "-ing,
Reproving her tears with " pooh-pooh "-ing and " tush "-
    ing.
    Then the serfs took away,
    And placed safe on the dray,
The casks which had held the material for lushing.

    Little more to be told,
    Of the miserly old
Baron Klopfzetterheim, rolling in gold.
    Of his beautiful Bertha
    He heard nothing further,
The clumsy old baron could never unearth her;
He ne'er could make out where his daughter had got to,
For of course he knew nothing at all about Otto.
From the date of the wedding he didn't live long;
Everything, after she left him, went wrong.

He broke a blood-vessel, endeavouring to bless (or
To curse—I don't know which) Miss Bertha's successor
(Appointed a few hours after she quitted),
Because accidently she omitted
His slippers to warm—he was much to be pitied!
    He broke a big blood-vessel up in his head,
    And fell on the floor of his palace, as dead
    As Otto's big brothers deep down in the cellar,
    And his fortune descended to Bertha la bella.

    Few hours they tarried
    Before they got married
In private—no bridesmaids, or breakfasts, or fitnesses;
The clerk and the pew-opener were the witnesses;
The bride (though in stuff) looked a beauty bewilderin';
They lived many years and had hundreds of childerin.

DOWN TO THE DERBY

(With Rhymes on the Road)

Waggon and cart, ready to start,
   Early in morning at six six;
Gallons of beer, stowed away here,
   Twiggery, swiggery, quick sticks.
Empty before, fill 'em once more;
   Women look trim in their caps, caps
Screaming in fun, never say done,
   Joking and poking the chaps, chaps.
Sweeps in a truck, swells out of luck,
   Laughery, chaffery, grin, grin;
Travelling show, dwarf hid below,
   Eye on his giantess' gin, gin.

Down to the Derby

Twiggery, swiggery, shinery, finery, laughery, chaffery,
    pokery, jokery;
Down to the Derby as all of us go,
These are the sights that we each of us know;
Yet off to the Downs as we often have been,
Still every year is some novelty seen.

Ten of the clock, carriages flock
   Round to the doors at the West-end;
People who seem, skimming the cream,
   To have laid hold of life at the best end
Phaeton and pair, baronet there,
   Lovely young girl with a smile, smile;
Look all about, splendid turn out,
   Everything done in good style, style.
Hampers retain lots of champagne,
   Hungerly, vulgarly, prog, prog,
Nothing more seek, nice little shriek,
   Missing him, kissing him, dog, dog.

Flunkeydom, monkeydom, finery, whinery, livery, shivery,
    fowlery, growlery—
Down to the Derby as all of us go,
These are the sights that we each of us know;
Yet off to the Downs as we often have been,
Still every year is some novelty seen.

Clapham we pass, schools in a mass,
   Up at the windows we go by
Playful as mice, governess nice,
   Thinkery, winkery, oh, fie!
Balham the dull vote it a mull,
   Marchery, starchery, slow, slow;

Down to the Derby

Tooting the next, sticks to its text,
    Travelly, gravelly, oh! oh!
Sutton a whet, thirsty we get,
    Palery, alery, take, take;
Smart four-in-hand comes to a stand,
    Legs of the longest ones ache, ache.

Drinkery, winkery, palery, alery, laughery, chaffery, crash
        along, dash along—
Down to the Derby as all of us go,
These are the sights that we each of us know;
Yet off to the Downs as we often have been,
Still every year is some novelty seen.

Trudging along, two dozen strong,
    Wearily, drearily, riff-raff,
Swells at them stare, singing the air
    Of Saturday's opera, " Piff paff."
Handful of coin all of them join,
    Rambling, scrambling, pick up;
Rowing for more, won't have " encore,"
    Frightening, tightening, stick up.
Posturers two come into view,
    Rummer set, summerset throwing;
Over they turn (don't try and learn),
    All that they get for it owing.

Palery, alery, smoking, jokery, rambling, scrambling, crash
        along, dash along—
Down to the Derby as all of us go
These are the sights that we each of us know;
Yet off to the Downs as we often have been,
Still every year is some novelty seen.

Down to the Derby

Under the trees, beautiful breeze,
   Lilacs in blossom we smell, smell;
May at last out (long while about),
   Country looks charming we tell, tell.
Everything seen, looking so green,
   Picture of verdure and so on;
Wonder if we green too, shall be,
   As to the horse we should go on.
Pike and " no trust," up comes the dust—
   Pay away, dray away, got, got;
Dustman before, oaths by the score,
   Fit for the drawing-room not, not.

Flurrying, worrying, holloing, following; lay away, pay
     away, crash along, dash along—
Down to the Derby as all of us go,
These are the sights that we each of us know;
Yet off to the Downs as we often have been,
Still every year is some novelty seen.

Epsom at last, nearing it fast,
   Smackery, crackery, whip, whip;
There's the Grand Stand, now close at hand,
   Think it a nice little trip, trip.
Get a good view, this one will do,
   Squeezing it, seizing it, rush, rush;
Downs looking smooth, CARELESS's Booth,
   Go in and get a good brush, brush.
Every one here, seems to appear,
   " How d'ye do? " " How are you? " nod, nod,
Some friends about, can't find 'em out,
   Look for them, hook for them, odd, odd.

Down to the Derby

Smackery, snackery, scenery, greenery, Leger bit, hedge a
        bit, look about, shook about—
Down to the Derby as all of us go,
These are the sights that we each of us know;
Yet off to the Downs as we often have been,
Still every year is some novelty seen.

Now take your place, this is the race,
   Universe, tune a verse, fame, fame;
Cards to be sold, everything told,
   Colours of riders and name, name.
Buzz! off they go, galloping so,
   Bothery, dothery, eye, eye;
Look as they pass, out with the glass,
   Can't find the focus to spy, spy.
Yonder they run, some horse has won,
   Up with the number and see, see;
Whichever is in, hundreds may win,
   But thousands will diddled like me be.

Cantering, bantering, cheering 'em, nearing 'em, spy away,
        fly away, dothery, bothery—
Down to the Derby as all of us go,
These are the sights that we each of us know;
Yet off to the Downs as we often have been,
Still every year is some novelty seen.

Derby complete, something to eat;
   Out with the provender, crush, crush;
Somebody walks, off with the forks,
   Bring out the bottles and lush, lush.
Plenty of pie, salad is nigh,
   Lettuces, let us seize, cool, cool;

Down to the Derby

Popkins an ass, broken a glass,
    Grittling, victualling, fool, fool;
Take to the wine, your health and mine,
    Drinkery, thinkery, nice, nice;
Off with the cup, finish it up,
    Sopping it, mopping it, trice, trice.

Readily, saidily, rather unsteadily, trickling, prickling.
    toiletty, spoiletty—
Down to the Derby as all of us go,
These are the sights that we each of us know;
Yet off to the Downs as we often have been,
Still every year is some novelty seen.

Stroll on the course—one of the force,
    Piping and wiping his brow, now;
Handkerchief missed, called to assist,
    Robbery, bobbery, row, row.
Off with a watch, guard but a botch,
    Tickery, quickery, fled, fled;
Fortune to tell, know it too well,
    Gipsying, tipsying, head, head.
Ground seems to turn, throat seems to burn,
    Whirl about, twirl about, steer clear;
Find out the drag, quizzed by a wag,
    Jokery, smokery, queer, queer.

Robbery, bobbery, watchery, botchery, dangling, wrang-
    ling, mumbling, grumbling—
Down to the Derby as all of us go,
These are the sights that we each of us know;
Yet off to the Downs as we often have been
Still every year is some novelty seen.

Down to the Derby

Eaten a snack, time to be back,
   Hurrying, scurrying, start, start;
Road as before, crammed but the more,
   With carriage and phaeton and cart, cart.
Out come the stars, light up cigars,
   Brandy and soda you must, must;
Road dry again, where was the rain?
   Smokery, chokery, dust, dust.
Come to a block, just at " The Cock,"
   Famous inn, same as in past time;
Pale ale to boot, take a cheroot,
   " Dal be, it shall be the last time."

Hurrying, scurrying, hampering, scampering, smokery,
      jokery, crash along, dash along—
Up from the Derby as all of us go,
These are the sights that we each of us know;
Yet off to the Downs as we often have been,
Still every year is some novelty seen.

Come to a pike, just what you like,
   Ticketing, stick it in, stop, stop;
Plenty of fun, never say done,
   Hattery, flattery, drop, drop.
Driving along, " let's have a song,"
   Mystery, history, none, none;
Dozens of keys, take which you please,
   Blowing horns, showing horns—Lon-don.
Lamps down the road, near your abode,
   Flare away, glare away, far, far;
Kennington-gate, longer to wait,
   Loud din and crowding at bar, bar.

Down to the Derby

Ticketing, stick it in, hattery, battery, flare away, stare
     away, splashery, dashery—
Up from the Derby as all of us go,
These are the sights that we each of us know;
Yet off to the Downs as we often have been,
Still every year is some novelty seen.

Home get at last, going it fast,
  Lifery, wifery, look, look;
Had no excess, buy a new dress,
  Made it all right with your " book, book."
Wake the next day, think of the way,
  How will the debts you incur be;
Or more to your mind, glad that you find,
  You did pretty well on the Derby.
Anyhow you think it will do,
  Not going now to be vexed here;
Hoping to spend with a " party " or friend,
  A holiday, jolly day, next year.

Theatre, be at a, upper rooms, supper rooms, choppery,
     moppery, steakery, rakery, singing too, bringing too,
     holiday, jolly day;
Fun thus we see as of old on the road,
This is the channel through which it has flowed;
Often to Epsom as people have been,
These are the fancies that freshen the scene.

THE PHANTOM HEAD

THERE never was a face
  So suited, in its way,
A clergyman to grace
  As MR. PARKS', M.A.
There never was a face
  (Excepting MR. PARKS')
More suited to its place,
  Than MR. PARKS's clerk's.

There never was a face
  So medically fine,
So free from metal base
  As that of DR. BRINE.
In fact, if actors could
  Contrive to " look a part "
As perfectly, they would
  Have mastered half their art.

These worthy people three
  They were the special pride
Of Twipton-on-the-Sea
  And all that country-side.
And strangers who might be
  In Twipton, too, would say,

The Phantom Head

" We never noticed three
　So *comme il-faut* as they."

But, ah, and well-a-day!
　I fear it wasn't meant,
That with our feature's play
　We should be quite content!
The clergyman would say,
　" My face is far too mild,
Suggestive in its way
　Of quite a little child."

The doctor wished for eyes
　That, eagle-like, would pierce;
The little clerk, likewise,
　He wished to look more fierce.
(We must not be severe:
　We have our failings, all;
For none are perfect here
　On this terrestrial ball.)

One night when nearly dark
　(The wind was blowing hard),
It so befel, the clerk
　Passed through the cold church-yard.
And, lo! while treading there,
　The causeway of the dead
He saw in middle-air
　A Solitary Head.

" Now this," he mused, " is strange,
　And though I may be dense,
It's quite beyond the range
　Of my experience.

The Phantom Head

I've noticed heads before,
   Young, pretty, old, and plain;
But all, I'm nearly sure
   Had bodies in their train."

" Clerk," said that Phantom Head,
   " Do you admire my smile? "
The clerk politely said,
   " It is my favourite style.
Your eyes, with lightning pronged
   Quite pierce me through and through;
For many years I've longed
   To have a head like you! "

" To-morrow evening, halt,"
   The awful Spectre said,
" At yonder handsome vault
   And you shall have my head.
For I, and brothers two
   (You would not know our names),
Were all beheaded, through
   The wicked SECOND JAMES.

" We're weary of our beds,
   That merciless old hunks,
Preserved our little heads
   But burnt our little trunks.
(' Trunks,' you'll observe, stand for
   Our bodies—now no more—
Not our portmanteaux, nor
   The breeches that we wore.)

The Phantom Head

" So, sure as eggs are eggs,
　　We never shall stir out
Until we get some legs
　　On which to move about.
Go, tell your worthy friends
　　That if they'll lend us theirs,
'Twill serve their private ends
　　And help us from our lairs."

The doctor and the priest
　　Rejoiced to hear that day
That they, good men, at least
　　Might have their wilful way.
Now mark the sorry plight
　　Their envy brought them to:
They sought the vault that night—
　　The Head had told them true!

But though the faces there
　　Looked handsome in the light,
In point of fact they were
　　Unsuited to them, quite,
One handsome head, each friend
　　Assumed—and bore it thence;
But, ah, the fearful end!
　　But, ah, the consequence!

For none would take a pew
　　In Mr. Parks's church,
The Doctor's patients, too,
　　Have left him in the lurch!
The humble little clerk
　　Has no companions, when

The Phantom Head

He rises grim and stark
    To give his loud Amen!

MORAL

You'll learn this moral fit, That beauty, to the state
Of him who pays for it Should be appropriate.

THE UNDECIDED MAN

Air: " The Sugar Shop "

Of all the small annoyances that weight our mental
    buoyances,
No chaff or cold derision is so sad as indecision is—
It's ruined me, it's plain it has—through life it's been my
    bane, it has,
It's driven me insane, it has, as anyone can see!
    Oh my! the troubles and perplexities,
    Oh dear! that mar each little plan!
    Oh law! sufficient quite to vex it is,
    The short uncertain temper of an undecided man!

In bed each day a-dundering, I lie awake a-wondering,
(In sad uncertain doubt of it) by which side to get out of it,

The Undecided Man

For all I ever knew of 'em have sides (or feet in lieu of 'em)
They've generally two of 'em, as anyone can see!
    Oh my! the troubles and perplexities! etc.

I never went a marrying but single stopped a-tarrying,
Though lots of girls I've known, I have; been introduced
        and shown, I have,
But ne'er a one I've got of 'em—no single girl could spot
        of 'em,
There's such a plaguey lot of 'em, as anyone can see!
    Oh my! the troubles and perplexities! etc.

I've reached a decent time of life, and tired, nearly, I'm of
        life,
Whom ought I to enquire of what illness to expire of?
Most men appear to fall of 'em—the short of 'em, the tall of
        'em,
I cannot die of all of 'em, as anyone can see
    Oh my! perplexed and always wondering,
    Oh dear! ill-natured people say,
    Oh law! I'm like in all my blundering,
    A donkey hesitating 'tween two packages of hay!

THE CATTLE SHOW: HALF-CROWN DAY

(By a very Heavy Swell)

No! I'm not in the least democratic,
　I object to a mob and a crush,
My tastes are too aristocratic
　My way through a crowd to push.
So when to the cattle I take my way,
It's on either a crown or a half-crown day!

I *in toto* object to the " people,"
　They are always so shockingly rude,
E'en on men on society's steeple,
　Their sad vulgar remarks they'll intrude.
So you cannot wonder I'd rather pay
To see the show on a half-crown day.

The Cattle Show: Half-Crown Day

On the high-priced days *c'est une autre*
   Chose tout à fait, if you please
Then the place is quite filled with *les notres*,
   With the people one everywhere sees,
Who, like myself, much prefer to pay
To see the show on a half-crown day.

Need I say that we don't care a button
   For the beasts in which farmer's delight;
As long as the sheep turn to mutton,
   And the oxen to beef, why it's right!
To see and be seen is for what we pay
At Islington on the half-crown day.

What to us are the tools used for farming?
   For our tenants they're all very well;
But there really cannot be a charm in
   Such things to the genuine swell.
And that being the case I prefer to pay
To see the show on a half-crown day.

THE CATTLE SHOW: THE SHILLING DAY

(By a very Low Fellow)

Pushing, crushing, panting, squeezing.
   Fat-faced farmers left and right;
Round the beasts scarce room for sneezing,
   Each one struggling for a sight.
That's the style, we like a mob,
And we've only paid a bob!

Into pigs umbrellas poking,
   Likewise sticks and parasols,
They're too fat to mind such joking,
   Thoughts of oil-cake fill their souls.
They are heedless of the mob
Who have only paid a bob!

Passing on, we next a visit
   To the fatted oxen make;
Prime indeed each sleek side is, it
   Makes us long to cut a steak.
Such things are not for the mob
Who have only paid a bob.

Then the sheep claim our attention,
   Southdowns, Devons, Herefords,

The Cattle Show: The Shilling Day

This a medal's gained, that, mention,
  Gladness bringing to their lords.
What care we? the vulgar mob
Who have only paid a bob!

To the implements for farming
  Next we turn, and drawing near,
Comes the thought there'd be no harm in
  Half a pie and bottled beer.
We eat and feel we're of the mob
Who have only paid a bob!

THE LADIES OF THE LEA

THERE was a flutter in the bosoms of the Ladies of the Lea,
When occurred a change of curates in their village by the
      sea;
For appointed to a living was the old BARTHOLOMEW,
And coming down to take his place, was JAMES, the curate
      new!

BARTHOLOMEW was reverend, but elderly and stout,
And a martyr to lumbago—he could scarcely get about;
But JAMES DE VYSE was young and fair, and comfortably off,
With the gentlest indication of a sweet consumptive cough.

His linen would have suited ALBERT EDWARD PRINCE OF
      WALES,
He was properly particular about his finger nails.
His legs were straight as arrows (as the picture of him shows),
His feet were little toddlekins, with tiddy-iddy toes.

Though anything but foppish, he was careful in his dress,
His trousers were perfection, his boots were nothing less.
I think he wore the smallest gloves of any man alive,
(His hand was barely seven, and his fingers only five).

The Ladies of the Lea

'Twas no unseemly vanity, but admiration meet,
Of Nature's skill as shown in abstract, hands, and legs, and feet.
He loved them for they proved that Nature only can combine,
Simplicity of outline with perfection of design.

It sprung from abstract reverence for Nature's Wondrous Touch:
Any feature in the Kosmos he'd have reverenced as much,
If any other feature had appeared to him as neat
As his pretty little legs, and little hands, and little feet.

And Jessie, Jane, and Margaret, the Ladies of the Lea,
When they heard that James de Vyse their future curate was to be,
Resolved to do whatever well-intentioned girls should do,
To atone for having slighted poor old fat Bartholomew.

Then Jessie (little Jessie!) thought, " How heedless have I been,
Of all religious duties, and in charity how mean!
I will mortify the body with fatiguing exercise,
I will work a pair of slippers for the Reverend de Vyse."

And Jenny, who for many months her parish work had shirked,
Exclaimed, " How have I slumbered, while devouter people worked!
Of penances and pains it's fit that I should suffer some,
I'll embroider pretty braces for the curate that's to come! "

The Ladies of the Lea

And Maggie said, " Oh, sluggish one! " (alluding to herself)
" How long shall works of piety lie idle on the shelf?
Lest Reverend De Vyse should think my toil a hollow form,
I will knit a pair of gloves to keep his jack-a-dandies warm! "

But Jessie, who at needlework was rivalled once by few,
Had grown quite out of practice during old Bartholomew:
And when the High Church slippers were delivered to De
Vyse,
They were very well intended but preposterous in size.

And Jenny, who for old Bartholomew had never toiled,
Found her schemes for decorating young De Vyse were
nearly foiled;
Want of practical experience with braces sent her wrong.
It was very kind of Jane, but they were very much too long.

And Maggie's want of practice told upon her efforts, too,
She had never knitted anything for old Bartholomew.
The gloves were kindly meant, but they were clumsy as
could be.
Poor Maggie did her best—but they were big enough for
me!

And did De Vyse reject these gifts because misfitting? No.
He wore them conscientiously, determining to show
That curates should endeavour (though with awkward
presents curst)
To conciliate parishioners—at all events at first.

And Jessie, Jane, and Margaret, the Ladies of the Lea,
Were eager all their presents on the Curate for to see;

The Ladies of the Lea

So they clambered up his garden wall, in three successive
    lifts,
And there was JAMES a-gardening in all his little gifts.

But the slippers, very roomy, made his feet appear a size
That caused both JANE and MARGARET unqualified surprise.
And the gloves that MAGGIE knitted in her leisure, I declare,
Were more like boxing gloves than those that curates ought
    to wear.

And the braces, though he triced them up as short as they
    could go
Left his trousers very baggy—anything but *comme il faut*;
They might have been suspended on a pair of wooden pegs,
So completely did they muffle all the drawing of his legs.

And JESSIE (who had laboured at the slippers on his feet)
Said, " His trotters, I allow you, are particularly neat,
But such coarse ungainly hands possess no interest for me,
And his legs are just as clumsy as a pair of legs can be! "

Then JENNY (who had made the pretty braces for him)
    spoke,
" I do *not* believe his legs deserve the comments they provoke;
But I quite agree his hands are very awful in their way,
And his feet! oh goodness gracious, what monstrosities are
    they! "

And MAGGIE (who had knitted the unhappy pair of gloves),
Said, " His hands too big? Oh, nonsense! Why, his hands
    are perfect loves!
But I quite agree with JENNY that his feet would suit a boor,
And I quite agree with JESSIE that his legs are very poor."

The Ladies of the Lea

So JESSIE, JANE, and MARGARET, the Ladies of the Lea,
Were satisfied that JAMES was as ungainly as could be;
They never quite recovered from their disappointment sore,
So they all became Dissenters, and he never saw them more!

MORAL

Young ladies, if you wish to marry curates, *don't refuse*
To work at gloves and slippers, e'en for old BARTHOLOMEWS;
Or your hands will lose their cunning, and you'll dis-
    appointed be,
Like JESSIE, JANE and MARGARET, the Ladies of the Lea.

SIR CONRAD AND THE RUSTY ONE

A KNIGHT for doughty doings rife,
   With falchion, lance, or bill,
Was fair SIR CONRAD TALBOTYPE,
   Of Talbotypetonneville.

His parents he had never known
   (The sting of many a taunt);
He had one relative alone—
   A sweet, dyspeptic aunt.

A time must come when loving hearts
   Must part awhile—and lo!
SIR CONRAD into foreign parts
   As errant-knight must go!

39

Sir Conrad and the Rusty One

Some name to which he might be true
   He sought for near and far,
But with the maidens whom he knew
   He was not popular.

Men jeered the knight who ne'er had been
   With love of maiden blessed,
Till, mad with disappointment keen,
   His aunt he thus addressed:

" No longer shall such chaff inane
   Against my head be hurled;
If you'll allow me, I'll maintain
   Your charms against the world!

" All knights shall at thine honoured name
   In fealty bend the knee—
From every errant I will claim
   His homage, aunt, for thee! "

A tear stood in her widow'd eye,
   And thus outspoke the dame—
" Oh, don't you think you'd better try
   Some younger lady's name?

" For folks would chuckle if they should
   Discover I'm your aunt——"
" I would," said CONRAD, " if I could,
   But, then, you see, I can't."

" Then go, my boy, with dauntless eye,
   My peerlessness maintain;

Sir Conrad and the Rusty One

Make this your dreaded battle-cry,
  ' KING HARRY and AUNT JANE! ' ''

     *   *   *   *   *

" Ho! stand, Sir Knight, if thou be brave,
  And try thy might with mine,
Unless you wish this trusty glaive
  To cleave thee to the chine! "

So spake SIR CONRAD as he thrust
  His lance in gallant mode—
Towards a knight in suit of rust,
  Who passed him on the road.

The knight at words so boldly shaped
  Stopped short and turned him round,
Then humbly touched his brow, and scraped
  His foot upon the ground.

" Ha! " quoth SIR CONRAD, " malapert!
  Dost think with threats to brave
SIR CONRAD's wrath, thou thing of dirt—
  Thou braggadocio knave?

" SIR CONRAD thus you may not daunt,
  Or make him hold his rein—
Come—swear you never knew an aunt
  So fair as my AUNT JANE! "

" Fair, sir," the Rusty One replied,
  " Indeed, I do not think
I ever knew but one—who died,
  And all along of drink."

41

Sir Conrad and the Rusty One

" Then own, thou braggart, by thy star,"
    SIR TALBOTYPE replied,
" That my AUNT JANE is fairer far
    Than she who lately died! "

The knight rejoined, " Oh, do not cut—
    Forbear, my lord, to strike!
I have not seen the lady, but
    I think it's very like.

" To that belief—I own it free—
    I solemnly incline—
No aunt of your's could ever be
    So great a beast as mine.

" She figured in Police reports
    Along of ' heavy wet,'
And was be-known at all the Courts
    As ' Coxybogy BET '! "

" Then sign this paper," CONRAD said,
    " Or there I'll stretch thee stark! "
The Rusty One inclined his head
    And made his knightly mark.

" Beshrew me! here's a dullard wight,
    Gramercy, halidame!
Thou call'st thyself an errant knight,
    And canst not sign thy name! "

" A knight? " exclaimed the Rusty One;
    " Lor' bless your honour, no!

Sir Conrad and the Rusty One

I'm only hired till set of sun
  To join the LORD MAYOR's SHOW! "

    *   *   *   *   *

SIR CONRAD hied him home again
  As quickly as he could,
Right-welcomed by his kind AUNT JANE
  And all the neighbourhood.

He told them how, in foreign land,
  He fought that rusty buck;
And though the maidens scorn his hand,
  They do not doubt his pluck.

CROQUET: AN ANTICIPATION

SHOULD the weather improve still, by Hokey,
We soon shall be playing at croquet!
Yes, knocking the balls, from the dawn
'Till the gloaming, all over the lawn,
Inviting our friends and our neighbours
To share in the pleasures and labours.
And first there'll be young MR. LUKEING
Who is terribly given to fluking;
And LAURA DE PIPPERY COOPER
We call her " the pitiless scooper,"
Because she so spoons, and so scoops,
In putting the balls through the hoops;

44

Croquet; An Anticipation

And then there's PENELOPE ARRABIN,
Whose brooch there's a strange-looking scarab in,
(Not that her brooch will a beetle be,
But the rhyme this the sole way to treat'll be);
And there is YOUNG COBB, who *will* try
To play with that glass in his eye,
But manages always to drop it
When he's making his stroke, and can't stop it;
And there's SPOONY, who hits the wrong ball,
And MISS MUFF who can't hit one at all;
MISS SPRY, who's a player expert,
If she only consents not to flirt;
And MISS KEEN who has got a sly way
Of pretending she really can't play,
That CAPTAIN DE BOOTS—" splendid cweacher! "
May gallantly offer to teach her;
Old MISS STIFFLER who thinks croquet " nice "—
(If not watched she will hit her ball twice);—
And that amiable MOLE, who's short-sighted,
And to trip o'er the hoops seems delighted;—
There'll be these, and a great many more,
I could soon swell the list to a score,
Or at least to a couple of dozen—
And la!—I forgot, there's my cousin—
   FRED—whose play may be always relied on,
It's odd that I'm always his side on!

THE SCORNFUL COLONEL

THOUGH not, as common rumour says,
Remarkable in other ways,
No haughty supercilious swell
Could scorn so well as COLONEL BELL.

46

The Scornful Colonel

At sight of snobs his lip would curl—
His lip would quiver, twist, and twirl
In an astonishing degree—
He often curled his lip at me.

His men, to give them all their due,
Were most accomplished sneerers, too:
Their Colonel gave them, with a will,
Six daily hours of sneering drill.

" Now, by your right, prepare to ' Whish '!
Come, all at once and smartly, ' Pish '!
Prepare to ' Bah '! By sections, ' Phew.'
Good! At three hundred yards, ' Pooh-pooh! ' ' "

And though (as I can prove too well)
They could not sneer like COLONEL BELL,
Still, not to flatter them a jot,
They were a supercilious lot.

Some two-and-thirty years ago
He sailed to fight the Paynim foe,
For then a dreadful war began
'Tween England and the Ottoman.

Once, going round his daily beats
In Stamboul's uninviting streets,
He heard these words, in accents clear,
" Oh, Little Stranger, welcome here! "

The Colonel stopped—he had no choice,
For, ah! it was a WOMAN's voice!
And through a window dark and grim
Two EYES flashed, lightning-like, on him.

The Scornful Colonel

Such eyes! So soft—so full of soul!
Such silent pathos in their roll!
No deadlier weapon women wield:
Au reste, her face was quite concealed.

" Oh, sir," the vision whispered, " though
You're certainly our country's foe
Let's hail the emblematic dove
As subjects of One Monarch—Love! "

" Oh, ma'am," he said—I will not stay
To tell you all he chose to say;
But all the workings of his brain
Were in the same impassioned strain.

" Oh, sir," the eyes replied, " I fear,
You dare not penetrate up here—
I'm no mere drab in humble life,
I *was* the Sultan's favourite wife! "

" Oh, *ma'am*! ! ! " said he—suffice to add,
The gallant Colonel, rapture-mad,
This graceful sentiment displays
In fifty-seven different ways.

He sought the Hareem's portals wide,
He sneered the sentinel aside,
And when his scornful eyeballs flashed,
The very guard fell back abashed!

On cloth of gold in *négligé*,
The Sultan's former fancy lay;
He saw that once (in early life)
She *might* have been his favourite wife.

The Scornful Colonel

ZARLINE (her name) with one big bound,
Threw COLONEL BELL her arms around,
And danced her best, but truth to tell,
She was a creaky, old gazelle.

The Colonel gazed—then turned away;
Love *fled*, and Duty held its sway:
That sterner stuff that, near and far,
Makes British warriors what they are.

" WHY BELL, my boy, come, come, what's this?
Unmanned by thoughts of simple bliss?
Unsoldiered by a lovely girl? "
The warrior's lip resumed its curl.

But ah, too late. The Sultan's ears
Much sharpened by his jealous fears,
Had overheard, behind a screen,
The creakiness of fair ZARLINE!

The Colonel soon was seized and bound;
He struggled not, but looked around,
Relying on the wide-spread fear
Instilled by his notorious sneer.

But ah! the move was ill-designed;
The Sultan he was old and blind,
And all the Hareem's soldiers then
Were elderly, short-sighted men!

Those soldiers soon contrived to pack
The gallant Colonel in a sack;
But, mindful of his scornful fame,
LIEUTENANT-COLONEL BELL died game.

The Scornful Colonel

The Bosphorus, with gloomy roll,
Closed mournfully upon his soul;
Its billows sang the only knell
That mourned LIEUTENANT-COLONEL BELL!

THE POLICEMAN'S BEARD

Go search throughout the human kind,
I'll undertake you will not find
A kinder, softer-hearted boy
Than gentle-eyed POLICEMAN JOY.

He sickened at the sight of sin,
And sought a hallowed refuge in
That haven of unruffled peace
The Metropolitan Police.

" Here," thought the gentle-minded lad,
" Protected from examples bad,
And far removed from worldly strife,
I'll pass a calm monastic life.

" For wicked men, with nimble feet,
Avoid the good policeman's beat;
And miscreants of every kind
Disperse like chaff before the wind.

" My beat shall serve me, as, I'm told,
Grey cloisters served the monks of old;
A spot convenient where at ease,
To ruminate on vanities.

The Policeman's Beard

" 'Twill be, on all material scores,
A monastery out-of-doors,
With (here it beats monastic shades)
A good supply of servant maids."

Nor did his hopes betray the boy,
His life was one unruffled joy,
He breathed, at Government's expense
An atmosphere of innocence.

Vice fled before him day by day,
While Virtue often " asked the way ";
Or beg he'd kindly leave his beat
To help her cross a crowded street.

Where'er he went 'twas just the same;
Whene'er he whistled, Virtue came;
And Virtue always found him near,
When she was sent to fetch the beer.

For Virtue said, " That gentle eye
Could never compass villainy.
A DON GIOVANNI none could trace
In that fair smooth angelic face! "

And Virtue guessed the simple truth,
He *was* a good and harmless youth,
As simple-hearted as he looked,
His " inside places " Truth had booked.

But, ah, alas! as time rolled on,
LIEUTENANT COLONEL HENDERSON
This order to policemen gave,
" All Constables must Cease to Shave! "

The Policeman's Beard

The order soon was noised about,
The prisoned beards broke madly out.
And sacred from the morning knife,
They revelled in a new-found life.

Moustachios, freed from scissor-clips,
Poured madly over upper-lips;
Or curled themselves in either eye—
They breathed the breath of Liberty!

How fared it with our gentle boy,
That tender lad, POLICEMAN JOY,
Whose eye recalls the mild gazelle?
Alas! with him it fared not well.

Attracted by no whistled air,
Shy shrinking Virtue took good care
To see the boy was no where near,
When she was sent to fetch the beer.

And Vice that used to run away
Would now take heart of grace, and say
" A beard that twirls and tangles thus
Must appertain to one of us! "

He brushed it often—combed it through,
He oiled it and he soaped it too;
But useless 'twas such means to try,
It curled again when it was dry.

Well, Virtue sadly gave him up,
Vice proffered him her poisoned cup,
And thus good, kind POLICEMAN JOY,
Became a lost abandoned boy!

The Policeman's Beard

That peaceful chin—those chubby cheeks,
That mouth that smiles, but rarely speaks,
Now wear by HENDERSONIAN law,
The fiercest beard you ever saw!

It spoke of blood—it spoke of bones,
It spoke of yells and midnight groans;
Of death in lonely robber-cribs,
Of poignards stuck between the ribs!

And Virtue, timid fluttering maid,
Shrank from her gentle boy afraid;
And took him for—I know not what,
At all events she knew him not.

WOMAN'S GRATITUDE

IN underbred society
  (Which I was nurtured in)
No species of impiety
  Is reckoned such a sin—
No shocking inhumanity
  So lowly to degrade
(Alas, oh, human vanity!)
  As being badly made.

Men, absolute iniquity
  With bandiness assess,
And physical obliquity
  With moral twistiness.
There, natural deformity
  Or curvature of bone
Is viewed as an enormity
  No penance can atone.

No atom of mortality
  Bore worthier repute,
For vigorous morality
  Than MR. BAKER COOTE.
Conspicuous for charity
  And active virtue, too—

Woman's Gratitude

In truth a moral rarity—
    A worthy man, and true.

But, ah, my friends, unluckily
    His form was strongly warped!
He bore his sorrow pluckily
    And seldom on it harped.
At parties, girls, perchance, with him
    Would nothing have to do—
No maiden cared to dance with him,
    Much less, of course, to woo.

Too short his legs were thought to be;
    His little back, no doubt,
Was higher than it ought to be;
    His arms, at times, slipped out.
One eye adored astronomy
    And bright celestial zones,
The other (strange economy!)
    Inspected paving stones.

Misshapen though amazingly
    With inconvenient twirl,
He dared to mention praisingly
    The bowyer WILSON's girl.
Grotesque as a barbarian
    (Poor BAKER COOTE, I mean)
He dared to love fair MARIAN,
    The Beauty of Wood-Green.

Although in form inferior
    He had affections fine—
A sensitive interior
    Like yours, dear friend, or mine

Woman's Gratitude

He dared to love the Beautiful,
 The Graceful, and the True,
The Sensible, the Dutiful,
 The Kind, and Well-to-do.

But she (poor COOTE in talking with,
 She banished all his claims)
Preferred to go out walking with
 A well-made person—JAMES.
Poor COOTE determined pluckily
 To stab that well-made man,
But incidents unluckily
 Occurred to baulk his plan.

So COOTE, with strange temerity
 Would gaze on her all day,
Till JAMES, with much asperity,
 Would bid him go away.
" Don't shorten my felicity,"
 Said BAKER in a blaze,
" The cat of domesticity
 On Royalty may gaze.

" Look on yon sky's concavity,
 The sun, celestial ball,
We, spite of our depravity,
 May love and worship all!
The moon shines brightly—beamingly—
 And though I'm crooked, it's true,
Yet I may court her, seemingly,
 Till everything is blue! "

JAMES, though adored by MARIAN,
 Was pitiably dense,

Woman's Gratitude

A common-place vulgarian
   With no poetic sense.
" Now, BAKER, go your ways, my boy,
   You poor, misshapen loon—
Spend, if you like, your days, my boy,
   In crying for the moon.

" Perhaps she is—you say she is—
   Unangered at your smiles,
But think how far away she is—
   Three hundred thousand miles!
Were you a gay Lunarian
   You might, I'm sure, have stared
All day at MISTRESS MARIAN
   For anything I cared! "

No man of true nobility
   Could stand such taunts and names,
Or suffer with tranquillity
   The gibes of well-made JAMES.
He used his blade unskilfully—
   With blunderbuss instead,
He aimed at JAMIE, wilfully,
   And shot that springald dead!

You would have fancied, tearfully,
   He would not sigh in vain,
Who braves the gallows cheerfully
   His only love to gain.
Don't let such wild insanity
   Upon your thoughts intrude,
You little know the vanity
   Of female gratitude!

THE "BANDOLINE" PLAYER

A TROUBADOUR, young, brave, and tall,
   One morning might be seen,
A singing under COLTER's hall
   Upon the village green,

He went through all the usual forms,
   And rolled his eyes of blue,
As dying ducks in thunderstorms
   Are often said to do.

For COLTER had a daughter, she
   Was barely twenty-two.
Why sang that minstrel party? He
   Adored her—so would you.

The "Bandoline" Player

He played upon a what's-it's-name—
  You know the thing I mean—
The *Pall Mall* critics call the same
  A " dainty bandoline."

And COLTER's daughter, wrapt in joy
  (A sweet, romantic maid),
She smiled upon that guileless boy
  As gracefully he played.

" Oh, person in the crimson legs,"
  She modestly exclaimed,
" A bashful maiden coyly begs
  You'll tell her how you're named.

" For, oh, you feed a tender flame
  In playing on the green,
And, oh, she loves what critics name
  The dainty bandoline! "

That troubadour he tore his hair
  And sent a sigh above,
To think his bandoline should share
  That maiden's wealth of love.

He hied him to his village shed,
  Wept village tears in quarts,
Then laid him on his village bed,
  And thought these village thoughts:

" I must be worshipped all in all,
  For what I've always been—
And not for what the critics call
  My dainty bandoline.

The "Bandoline" Player

" To which of us her loving may
  Be due, I'll thus detect—
Upon the fiddle I can play
  With singular effect.

" To-morrow, with its graceful aid,
  Her moments I'll beguile,
That maiden I will serenade
  In JOACHIM's finest style."

And so he did, that gallant boy,
  But never came the maid:
He, hoping she was only coy,
  Still sang to her and played.

BEETHOVEN, GLUCK, PICCINI, SPOHR,
  He gave her for a while,
And other masters, even more,
  " Dot-touch-and-go " in style.

For hours that patient boy he played
  At FATHER COLTER's farm—
Behind his noble shoulder-blade,
  And underneath his arm:

Below his leg—behind his back
  He played till he was red—
Between his knees, with dainty knack,
  And then above his head.

With musico-gymnastic tricks
  He warbled forth her name:
From half-past nine till half-past six,
  But, ah! no maiden came.

The "Bandoline" Player

(For MARY had been sent away
  To Weston-super-Mare—
A fact of which that minstrel gay
  Was wholly unaware.)

But FATHER COLTER rose at nine,
  His wrath it also rised,
For fiddle, voice, and bandoline
  He equally despised.

" I have," said he, " some bellows *here*—
  A fine young noddle *there*—
It would but be politeness mere
  To introduce the pair! "

No sooner was it said than done,
  And as above I've shown,
Upon the sconce he fetched him one—
  One for himself alone!

" Ah, MARY," said the simple lad,
  " I know thy gentle touch,
Upon my word this is too bad,
  I feel it very much.

" That you don't care for me at all
  Is easy to be seen—
You love what *Pall Mall* critics call
  My dainty bandoline! "

(But MARY had been sent away
  To Weston-super-Mare—
A fact of which that minstrel gay
  Was wholly unaware.)

" EHEU! FUGACES "

An old man sitting in church, and praying with all his
    breath.
An old man waiting alone for the life that comes of death;
As the parson tells the well-worn tale of heaven and earth.
Of the life that is only death—of the death that is only birth!

Aye, he could patter it all by heart, as a school-boy hale;
But the old, old words are telling a new and a welcome
    tale.

"Eheu! Fugaces"

For the seal of death is set on the old man's wrinkled brow,
And words that once meant little are fraught with meaning
now.

Dead in a pauper's grave, long 'ere next Christmas day,
Here is the end at last—and it seemed so far away!
A careless wilful lad with many an idle plan—
A reckless headstrong youth—a cold indifferent man.

Much such a man as a dozen in thirteen are;
Day in the fields at work, and night in the ale-house bar.
Nor better nor worse than others, though oftener wrong
than right:
He worked with a will in the week, and he fought on
Saturday night.

Yet he was often at church, where he made believe to pray,
For the rector furrowed the land for many a mile away:
And the rector's smile meant work, and a home with plenty
crowned.
God help the fellow on whom that terrible rector frowned!

And often at church (for the parson proved a useful friend)
He listened perforce to the oft-told tale of the bad man's
end,
With a sulky frown on his face as he shuffled a restless limb:
He was young and merry and strong—such words were
never for him!

At times the turn of a hymn, or a simple Bible tale
Chimed with the voice of his soul—a low half-stifled wail—
And roused the frivolous man to a sense of sorrow and pain;
But the long dull sermon always hardened his heart again!

64

"Eheu! Fugaces"

The sermon's just as dull as it was in the days of yore;
But it bears a meaning now that it never possessed before:
The words are strange and long, but he knows their upshot
    well,
" The good will go to heaven—the wicked will go to hell! "

No scholar was he at his best, and his eyes are dim with age,
But the Book of the Earth is his, and he reads its open page,
Though rarely glanced at once, no longer idly scanned,
But there's little remains to read, for the end is close at hand.

In every silent page he finds a parable now;
In the plough that furrows the land—in the seed that follows
    the plough—
In the snow that covers the grass, and crackles under his
    tread—
In the grass that covers the mould—in the mould that
    covers the dead.

THE THREE BOHEMIAN ONES

A WORTHY man in every way
Was MR. JASPER PORKLEBAY:
He was a merchant of renown
(The firm was PORKLEBAY AND BROWN.)

Three sons he had—and only three—
But they were bad as bad could be;
They spurned their father's righteous ways.
And went to races, balls, and plays.

On Sundays they would laugh and joke,
I've heard them bet—I've known them smoke.
At Whist they'd sometimes take a hand,
These vices JASPER couldn't stand.

The Three Bohemian Ones

At length the eldest son, called DAN,
Became a stock tragedian,
And earned his bread by ranting through
SHAKSPERIAN parts, as others do.

The second (DONALD) would insist
On starting as a journalist,
And wrote amusing tales and scenes
In all the monthly magazines.

The youngest (SINGLETON his name)
A comic artist he became,
And made an income fairly good
By drawing funny heads on wood.

And as they trod these fearful ways
(These three misguided PORKLEBAYS),
They drew not on their father's hoard—
For JASPER threw them overboard.

Yes, JASPER—grieving at their fall—
Renounced them one—renounced them all;
And lived alone so good and wise
At Zion Villa, Clapham Rise.

By dint of work and skilful plan
Our JASPER grew a wealthy man;
And people said, in slangy form
That JASPER P. would " cut up warm."

He had no relative at all
To whom his property could fall,
Except, of course, his wicked sons,
Those three depraved Bohemian ones!

The Three Bohemian Ones

So he determined he would fain
Bequeath his wealth (despite Mortmain),
Freeholds, debenture stock, and all
To some deserving hospital.

When his intent was known abroad,
Excitement reigned in every ward,
And with the well-experienced throng
Of operators all went wrong.

St. George's, Charing Cross, and Guy's,
And little Westminster likewise,
And Lying-In and Middlesex,
Combined old JASPER to perplex.

House-surgeons, spite of patients' hints,
Bound head-aches up in fracture-splints;
In measles, strapped the spots that come,
With strips of plain diachylum.

Rare Leeches, skilled at fever beds,
For toothache shaved their patients' heads;
And always cut their fingers off
If they complained of hooping cough.

Their zeal grew greater day by day,
And each did all that with him lay
To prove his own pet hospital
The most deserving of them all.

Though JASPER P. could not but feel
Delighted at this show of zeal,
When each in zeal excels the rest,
One can't determine which is best.

The Three Bohemian Ones

Interea, his reckless boys
Indulged in low Bohemian joys,
They sometimes smoked till all was blue,
And danced at evening parties too.

The hospitals, conflicting sore,
Perplexed poor JASPER more and more,
But, ah, ere JASPER could decide,
Poor charitable man, he died!

And DONALD, SINGLETON, and DAN,
Now roll in wealth, despite his plan.
So DONALD, DAN, and SINGLETON,
By dint of accident have won.

Vice triumphs here, but if you please,
'Tis by exceptions such as these
(From probability removed)
That every standing rule is proved.

By strange exceptions Virtue deigns
To prove how paramount she reigns;
A standing rule I do not know
That's been more oft established so.

FANNY AND JENNY

FANNY and JENNY in Paris did dwell,
MISS JANE was a dowdy, MISS FANNY a swell—
Each went for to dine at a quarter to four
At her own little favourite Restauratore—
FANNY of BERTRAM AND ROBERTS was fond
While JENNY she worshipped her SPIERS AND POND.

FANNY was pretty and piquante and pert,
Her manners were shortish and so was her skirt,
While JENNY the elder would make a man wince,
In a dress of the mode of a century since.
BERTRAM AND ROBERT'S FANNY was blonde,
And dark was the JENNY of SPIERS AND POND.

Fanny and Jenny

JANE lived in a modest and lady-like way:
To SPIERS AND POND she went every day,
She'd order up beef and potatoes as well,
And cut off the joint until senseless she fell:
(She fed herself daily all reason beyond
To gaze all the longer at SPIERS AND POND.)

But FANNY, that frolicsome frivolous maid
(Whose tastes were more airy than JENNY'S the staid),
To BERTRAM AND ROBERTS would hie her away,
And swallow plum-pudding the rest of the day.
The best of her dresses MISS FANNY she donned
(As JENNY did also for SPIERS AND POND).

The Restaurateurs didn't seem for to care
For JENNY'S soft ogle or FANNY'S fond stare.
Said JENNY, " Don't let us be taken aback,
We're probably on an erroneous tack,
And BERTRAM AND ROBERTS of *me* may be fond,
While *you* are beloved by SPIERS AND POND! "

" Oh, BERTRAM AND R., are you dying for me,
Or am I the chosen of SPIERS AND P.?
Oh, which is the angel and fostering star
Of SPIERS AND P., or of BERTRAM AND R.,
Which firm have I collared in VENUS'S bond?
Say, BERTRAM AND ROBERTS—speak SPIERS AND POND!

" Perhaps if you cannot completely agree
Which of you shall have FANNY and which shall have me,
And you wish for to go for to do what is right,
You will go to the Bois de Boulogne for to fight—
It's the mode that is popular in the *beau monde*,—
Will BERTRAM AND ROBERTS fight SPIERS AND POND? "

Fanny and Jenny

But SPIERS AND POND are but perishing clay,
So they gasped and they gurgled and fainted away—
The burden of BERTRAM AND ROBERT'S song
Was " Goodness! how shocking! Oh, please go along!
With neither for worlds would we ever abscond! "
And " Ditto for us," exclaimed SPIERS AND POND.

Said FANNY, " How bold, and how dreadfully rude! "
" These men are too forward," said JENNY the prude.
" Such youth and such beauty as both of us own
Are safe in the walls of a convent alone,
We shall there be the coarse persecutions beyond
Of BERTRAM AND ROBERTS and SPIERS AND POND."

BLABWORTH-CUM-TALKINGTON

DRAPER's clerk in a humble way,
  Margate-bound, on a Seventh-day;
  Gent in figured dicky and frill
  Smoking pipes on Richmond Hill;
  Coster dressed for an Epping bout;
  Servant-gal with a Sunday out;
  Quail, quail, quail, quail!
  Here is the REVEREND BARNEY PAYLE,
    Good in a dismal way!
      Gurgle and groan
      Never were known
      Ever to fail
      BARNABY PAYLE,
    BARNABY PAYLE, B.A.

Blabworth-cum-Talkington

Rumble, blunder, stumble, thunder,
Wrangle, tangle, jingle-jangle,
Fluttery stuttery, bog, fog,
    Missing his tack,
    Changing his track,
    Losing his threads,
    Mixing his " heads,"
Flash! Dash! Splash! Crash!
Slowly, fastly, grimly, ghastly
Firstly, secondly, thirdly, lastly
    Lastly first,
    Firstly last,
    Sinners curst,
    Hope all past.
Down! down! down! down!
Sob—sigh—gulp—frown.
Boil! boil! boil! boil!
Boiling lead and blazing oil.
    Groans—squirms—
    Bones—worms—
Contradiction full, in terms,
    (Half-past one—
    Almost done).
Wake! wake! wake! wake!
    Deuce to take!
    All at stake
Wake! wake! wake! wake!
Suddenly—grandly devotional—
Thrilling—emphatic—emotional—
    Various kinds
    Of baby minds
Trained on BARNABY PAYLE-ian rules,
At Blabworth-Talkington Infant Schools.
Fill, oh, fill the silver plate—

Blabworth-cum-Talkington

Donors dwindling down of late—
Hundreds wanted—thousands—more—
Give, oh, give at the church's door!

This was the sermon one fine day,
Preached by BARNABY PAYLE, B.A.,
The first he'd ever had to speak,
For PAYLE was only " frocked " last week.

In an otherwise empty pew,
Sat a respectable Jew,
His starting eyeballs glistened—
Despite dissent, with best attent
That Hebrew person listened.
And PAYLE, B.A., remarked the way
In which the Jew drank in, that day,
The burning things he chose to say,
And hoped to see him christened.

The sermon at an end
His Israelitish friend,
Heart-smitten to the core
Sought out the vestry door.
" Oh, admirable PAYLE,
I've heard my people rail
Against your priests, and say that they can only smirk or
    roar,
But I can only say
That, thanks to you, to-day
I've learnt a better lesson than I ever learnt before.

" I've learnt why clerks in a humble way
Sail abroad on their Seventh Day;

75

Blabworth-cum-Talkington

I've learnt why costermongers will
Spend that day on the Epping-hill;
I've learnt the meaning of pious cant,
Baldness, ignorance, dulness, rant—
A wonderful study for thoughtful minds
At Blabworth-Talkington Church one finds! "

THE STORY OF GENTLE ARCHIBALD

My children, once I knew a boy
(His name was Archibald Molloy),
Whose kind papa, one Christmas time,
Took him to see a pantomime.
He was a mild, delightful boy,
Who hated jokes that did annoy;
And none who knew him could complain
That Archie ever gave them pain.
But, don't suppose he was a sad,
Or serious, solemn kind of lad;
Indeed, he was a cheerful son,
Renowned for mild, respectful fun.

The Story of Gentle Archibald

But, Oh, it was a rueful day
When he was taken to the play;
The Christmas Pantomime, that night
Destroyed his gentle nature, quite;
And as they walked along the road
That led to his papa's abode,
As on they trudged, through mud and mire,
He said, " Papa, if you desire
My fondest hopes and joys to crown
Allow me to become a Clown! "
I will not here attempt to show
The bitter agony and woe,
The sorrow and depression dire
Of Archie's old and feeble sire.
" Oh, Archibald," said he, " my boy,
My darling Archibald Molloy!
Attention for one moment lend—
You cannot seriously intend
To spend a roving life in town,
As vulgar, base, dishonest clown.
And leave your father in the lurch,
Who always meant you for the Church,
And nightly dreams he sees his boy
The Reverend Archibald Molloy! "

That night, as Archie lay awake;
Thinking of all he'd take and break,
If he but had his heart's desire,
The room seemed filled with crimson fire;
The wall expanded by degrees,
Disclosing shells and golden trees,
Revolving round, and round, and round;
Red coral strewn upon the ground;
And on the trees, in tasty green,

The Story of Gentle Archibald

The loveliest fairies ever seen;
But one more fair than all the rest,
Came from a lovely golden nest,
And said to the astonished boy,
" Oh, Master Archibald Molloy,
I know the object of your heart—
To-morrow morning, you shall start
Upon your rambles through the town
As merry, mischief-making clown."

    *   *   *   *   *

Next day, when Nurse Amelia called,
To wash and dress her Archibald,
She opened both her aged eyes
With unmistakable surprise,
To find that Archie, in the night
Had turned all red, and blue, and white,
Of healthy colour, not a trace—
Red patches on his little face,
Black horsehair wig, round rolling eyes,
Short trowsers, of prodigious size,
White legs and arms, with spots of blue,
And spots upon his body, too!
Said she, " Why, what is this, my boy?
My gentle Archibald Molloy!
Your good papa I'll go and tell,
You must be dreadfully unwell,
Although I know of no disease
With any symptoms such as these."

The good old lady turned to go
And fetch his good papa, when lo
With irresistible attack
He jumped upon her aged back,

The Story of Gentle Archibald

Pulled off the poor old lady's front,
And thrashed her, while she tried to grunt,
" Oh, Archibald, what have you done?
Is this your mild, respectful fun,
You bad, ungentlemanly boy?
Fie on you, Archibald Molloy! "
Some dreadful power, unseen but near,
Still urged on his wild career,
And made him burn, and steal, and kill,
Against his gentlemanly will.
The change had really turned his brain;
He boiled his little sister Jane;
He painted blue his aged mother;
Sat down upon his little brother;
Tripped up his cousins with his hoop;
Put pussy in his father's soup;
Placed beetles in his uncle's shoe;
Cut a policeman right in two;
Spread devastation round—and, ah,
He red-hot-pokered his papa!

Be sure, this highly reckless course
Brought Archibald sincere remorse;
He liked a joke, and loved a laugh,
But was too well-behaved by half—
With too much justice and good sense—
To laugh at other folk's expense.
The gentle boy could never sleep,
But used to lie awake and weep,
To think of all the ill he'd done.
" Is this," said he, " respectful fun?
Oh, fairy, fairy, I would fain
That you should change me back again;

The Story of Gentle Archibald

Some dreadful power I can't resist
Directs my once respected fist;
Change, and I'll never once complain,
Or wish to be a clown again! "

He spoke, and lo! the wretched boy
Once more was Archibald Molloy;
He gave a wild, delighted scream,
And woke—for, lo, it was a dream!

TO MY ABSENT HUSBAND

TELL me, Edward, dost remember
How, at breakfast, often we
Put our bacon in the tea-pot
While we took and fried our tea?

How we went to evening parties
On gigantic brewer's drays,
How you wore your coats and trousers,
In those happy, happy days?

How we used to pocket ices,
When a modest lunch we bought?
Quaff the foaming Abernethy,
Masticate the crusty port?

To my Absent Husband

How we fished in deep sea water
For the barbel, tench and carp?
Wore our rings upon our pencils,
While we cut our fingers sharp?

How we cleaned our boots with sherry
While we drank the blacking dry?
How we quite forgot to pay for
Articles we used to buy?

How, a ruffian, prosecuting,
Who'd been swindled, so he said,
We appeared at the Old Bailey,
And were done, ourselves, instead?

THE BALLAD OF PLIGHTED LOVE

IF my anticipation's correct
   When I come to swoop down on my quarry,
That he treated my love with neglect
   I think he'll be certainly sorry!
I'll hide his dress-suits, and I'll put little brutes like black-
   beetles and newts in the toes of his boots;
When fatigued and half dead he shall sup on dry bread, and
   lay down his poor head on an apple-pie bed;
Then to add to his woes, all his socks and his hose shall be
   rubbish that goes at the heels and the toes;
His meat shall be tough, and he shan't have enough, and
   his pudding or puff shall be flavoured with snuff;
His claret, I think, in acidity pink will resemble red ink;
   and the coffee he'll drink,
As to flavour and smell you'll alone parallel in the stuff that
   they sell in a British hotel!
     He shall live, for his guilt,
     In a house jerry-built;
     All the chimneys shall smoke
     Till he's ready to choke;
     And the plaster shall fall
     Both from ceiling and wall;
The roof it shall leak, and the pipes shall congeal,
The doors they shall warp (being made of new deal),

The Ballad of Plighted Love

And the stucco shall mildew and blister and peel,
      And the chimney-pots rock to and fro—so.
    By his lease he'll be bound
    To make everything sound;
    So he'll put up oak doors,
    And lay down polished floors,
    Admiration excite
    With stained glass and lead light,
Red tiles and rough cast, matting dado and frieze
(He'll have caught the prevailing artistic disease,
Pompeian—Renaissance—Queen Anne—Japanese,
      And his taste is exceedingly so-so).
    Well, the rabble and rout
    Of bricklayers clear out;
    He has got rid of *them*,
    And his house is a gem,
    All his troubles are past,
    And he's happy at last—
When he feels an unpleasant abdominal pain,
With a taste in his mouth, and a throb in his brain:
Sewer-gas—nothing more—something wrong with the
    drain!
It is easily stopped—so the builders explain.
Very likely these gentry are right in the main,
But the antidote proves to be worse than the bane,
For it brings all the bricklaying plagues in its train:
The walls must come down, and that lets in the rain—
The clean Morris paper is covered with stain—
The new polished oak has brick-dust in its grain;
All the floors must come up, and remonstrance is vain
And the wretched householder is driven insane,
For he's got to do everything over again!

CRINOLINE ON THE ICE

WHAT prettier sight when our ponds are all frozen,
And skaters rush out to the parks by the dozen,
Than to see a sweet girl—her skates on in a trice—
Scud away in her crinoline over the ice?

There are many events the amusement to heighten,
Un Anglais timide it is easy to frighten!
And we all must admit it would scarcely be nice
To be carried by crinoline over the ice.

The shape of an ankle there's good chance of showing,
And eyes are most bright when with pleasure they're
     glowing

Crinoline on the Ice

Whilst rarely are charms more likely t'entice,
Than when whirling on crinoline over the ice.

Charming sensations, when crowds in gyrations,
Cut figures fantastic with wonderful patience;
And a perfect adept cuts an 8 in a trice,
Spite of crinoline sweeping all over the ice!

Jolly hours, too, for a winter flirtation,
In specious disguise of a wild recreation!
And we ask all the swells if they don't find it nice
To escort girls in crinoline over the ice.

There are slippings, and slidings, and various dilemmas;
If all KITTIES can skate, it's not so with all EMMAS;
And few are the girls who will care at what price
They venture in crinoline over the ice.

Winter is come with his locks long and hoary,
And ne'er will he leave us without the old story;
If there's one thing to give these short dull days a spice
It is skating in crinoline over the ice.

KING ARCHIBALD NASO

PRAY list to the story I'm going to tell
Of a monarch's most whimsical organ of smell;
For his fun and his frolic he'd only to tweak
The end of his famous fantastical beak.
And he split his old sides for a week and a day, so
Amused with his nose was KING ARCHIBALD NASO.

Whenever a subject, I'll venture to take
Any wager, miles off, was enjoying a steak,
He would say to his chamberlain, " Come! I'll be shot
If some villain ain't eating his steak with shallot.
I demand for that onion his head at a blow,
'Twon't suit this olfactory organ, you know!

They would have us believe in Arabian tales,
That a mountainous magnet drew ships of their nails,
But a fact, which is stronger, I certainly deem,
Occurred when KING ARCHIBALD walked by a stream;
Then the frogs and the lizards their pitches and tosses
Kept playing on ARCHIBALD's lengthy proboscis!

But the funniest freak which KING ARCHIBALD had
Was the wish to be everywhere known as a lad;

King Archibald Naso

He had chronic lumbago, rheumatics and gout,
He was wheezy, uneasy, dyspeptic and stout.
And yet though he coughed twenty times on the stairs,
He would still keep assuming most juvenile airs!

For years upon years he still kept on this track,
Of port and brown sherry he still took his whack,
But one morning he found to his utter dismay
That his wicked old nose had turned suddenly gray!
Then his friends sneaked away—many friends have this way
    —so
He fondled alone his old nose did KING NASO.

THE VARIABLE BABY

THERE never was a man
  Who studied more minutely
His very simplest plan
  Than JEREMIAH STUTELY.

The smallest of his schemes,
  (As I've already stated)
And all his wildest dreams,
  Were equally debated.

But, ah! of all the host
  Of social cons that harry,
This con perplexed him most,
  " Shall I do well to marry? "

The Variable Baby

For A. espoused a wife
   Young, lovely, and with money,
And people thought their life
   Would be one moon of honey.

But, ah! before a year
   O'er life's rough road they'd jolted,
With some disgraceful peer
   Good MRS. A. had bolted.

While B., whose wife is plain,
   Poor, cross, and half-demented,
Seems always, in the main,
   Exceedingly contented.

But there is C., his joy,
   (His wife, a year united,
Has given him a boy
   And C. is quite delighted.)

And STUTELY sees his pride,
   And thinks it pleasant, rather,
(And also dignified)
   To be a baby's father.

" But ah! " thinks he, " perhaps
   This baby, full of graces,
May prove the worst of chaps,
   And have the worst of faces!

" To-day's bright source of joy
   May joyless be to-morrow,
And this much-cherished boy
   May bring his parents sorrow!

The Variable Baby

" I'll see how he turns out,
　His parents' care rewarding,
A Crichton or a lout,
　And I'll be ruled according.

" If Baby turns out well,
　I certainly will marry—
If Baby proves a sell,
　A bachelor I'll tarry! "

Now, Baby's good as gold,
　With cheeks as red as roses,
And STUTELY (rather old)
　To some fair maid proposes:

Now, Baby's cross and cries,
　And won't let Nursey clean it;
And STUTELY seeks his prize,
　And says he didn't mean it.

Well, Baby, fat and bluff,
　And first-rate health enjoying—
Is sometimes good enough,
　And sometimes most annoying.

And S., with puzzled fate,
　Immediate marriage throws up,
And thinks he'd better wait
　And see how Baby grows up.

When Baby grows a lad
　No rule of conduct stops him;
And when extremely bad,
　His father comes and whops him.

The Variable Baby

And STUTELY says with joy,
  " I'm glad I thought of stopping;
I couldn't whop a boy,
  And boys want lots of whopping! "

When Baby grows a man
  He takes to serious teaching;
And later on, began
  A course of highway preaching.

And STUTELY cries " Well done!
  A credit to his mother!
That's something like a son—
  I wish I'd such another! "

And Instinct whispers " Mate!
  You're wasting time, you gaby! "
But Prudence whispers " Wait!
  And see what comes of Baby! "

And Prudence gains the day,
  For Baby takes to orgies:
He seeks the sinner's way,
  And finally he forges.

And Baby, for his crime,
  Is numbered, shaved and sorted,
And to a penal clime
  Is carefully transported.

And STUTELY shakes his head,
  And says he's glad he tarried;
And STUTELY's still unwed,
  And means to die unmarried.

BALLAD OF A NOBLE DUKE

I'M an excellent Duke in my way:
  I have picked up some tricks of gentility;
  I can talk with refined affability
To people of middle-class clay.
Without a suggestion of shame,
  I can throw off Society's fetters,
  And patronize science and letters;
Though I can scarcely spell my own name.
I can run, if I please, into debt
  (I know of some eminent Graces
  Who sit in conspicuous places
Who never paid any one yet).
My station exempts me from blame,
  And all the inferior classes
  (Whose charity nothing surpasses

94

Ballad of a Noble Duke

When they deal with a Duke) will exclaim—
  " You see, he's a person of rank;
  If he does now and then play a prank,
    He's a dashing young fellow,
    When older he'll mellow:
    So many temptations
    Unknown to our stations
  Beset a young fellow of rank! "

However addicted to range,
  I dispose of a dozen Church livings;
  And no one has any misgivings,
And no one considers it strange.
No question can ever arise
  That I cannot immediately settle,
  For peers of my popular mettle
Are born so exceedingly wise.
My expressions need never be minced;
  A duke is by nature omniscient.
  His simple opinion's sufficient,
And everybody's convinced.
His rank he may drag through the mud;
  If his lie is depravity's essence,
  After all, it's the mere effervescence
Of uncorked aërated blue blood—
  For, you see, he's a person of rank;
  If he does now and then play a prank,
    He's a dashing young fellow,
    When older he'll mellow;
    So many temptations
    Unknown to our stations
  Beset a young fellow of rank!

A. AND B.; OR, THE SENSATION TWINS

Once, under Spain's enfeebling sun,
  Twin brothers lived with me,
And, personality to shun,
  I call them A. and B.

They loved each other—that they did,
  'Twas rumoured near and far,
But from the time each was a kid
  Were most dissimilar.

A. had a pair of monstrous eyes,
  B.'s eyes were awful small;
B.'s nose attained a fearful size,
  A. had no nose at all.

A. and B.; or, the Sensation Twins

A.'s hair reached, when he shook it out,
   The middle of his leg;
B.'s little head was just about
   As bald as any egg.

B. had a thin and taper waist,
   A. had no waist at all;
A. was too short for proper taste,
   B. just as much too tall.

And for his benefit I say
   Who further knowledge seeks,
The one had Civil Service pay,
   The other wrote critiques.

They meekly bore their painful lots,
   Men shunned them as a cuss:
And little tiny todding tots
   Would babble at them thus:

" We don't believe you're human kind—
   We would not on your oath—
So unconceivably designed,
   Exaggerations both! "

And A.'d reply, " It's very true
   That I am much too short;
And B., I must admit that you
   Too tall by half are thought.

" But why this taunt from every curb,
   In bold defiance hurled?
The average we don't disturb—
   We wouldn't for the world!

A. and B.; or, the Sensation Twins

" If you complain we're badly planned,
   Why all you've got to do
Is, add us both together and
   Divide the sum by two! "

The notion pleased the simple lad,
   He thought it quaintly rare,
It soon became his favourite fad
   To sing it everywhere.

" Divide us, please! " they would exclaim,
   With unabated noise,
A mania it at length became
   With these afflicted boys.

A Turk there was—BEN OUSEFF named,
   An armourer by trade
(He was the maker of the famed
   " One shilling Damask blade.")

These lads their little joke would shout
   At peaceful OUSEFF's side,
And took delight in screaming out,
   " Divide us—pray, divide! "

The quaint conceit amused him much,
   He'd laugh, and would declare
With all his honest heart, that such
   A jest was passing rare!

Encouraged in their mirthful play
   They'd scream and yell and shout,
" Divide us, please! " till he would say,
   " Enough, my friends—get out."

A. and B.; or, the Sensation Twins

But still they screamed and would not list,
 " Divide us, monstrous men! "
" Well, since upon it you insist,
 I will," said honest BEN.

" Your joke is getting stale and trite,
 You shan't offend again."
And then he smote a mighty smite,
 And cleft them into twain!

They shammed no meretricious glee
 At OUSEFF's handiwork;
A. felt it very much, and he
 Said sternly to the Turk:

" This is a quibble, sir, and what
 Sharp practice people call— "
" It's what you asked for! " " No, it's not—
 By no means—not at all! "
  * * * * *
I often wish I knew how they
 Drain their unpleasant cup:
I only know that B. and A.
 Were terribly cut up.

Perhaps they lived in severed bliss—
 Perhaps they groaned and died—
Perhaps they joined themselves like this,
 And gave their legs a ride.

BOULOGNE

Of all the snug places where hard working races rush every
    summer, a crop of 'em,
I think you will own that delightful Boulogne may be said
    to stand quite at the top of 'em.
It's conveniently near, and it's not over dear, so your purse
    won't want much re-imbursing;
You can sit on a bench and learn how to speak French, just
    from hearing the natives conversing.
It has balls and two piers, and plump British young dears,
    and sands, theatre, picnics and races;
Then it's clean and it's bright, and, oh! different quite to
    our commonplace watering-places!
It was once two days' sail, but the South-Eastern mail goes
    so quick that it isn't thought, now, far.
You can say, too, you've been on the Continent seen—
    though, of course, you need never say how far!
        Though other towns can boast of crowns,
           I think you'll freely own,
        For bathing rare, and breezy air,
          There's nothing like Boulogne!

If you're French in your taste, you can pull in your waist,
    and imbibe, till all consciousness ceases,
Absinthe and Vermouth, with the Boulonnais youth, and
    play billiards like mad for franc pieces—

Boulogne

You can sit in a café with gents rather raffy—a weed in
      your teeth you can make fast,
And French training to show, take grapes, soup and
      Bourdeaux at twelve thirty, and call it a breakfast!
Or, if you incline to tea rather than wine (British dishes
      your mind, perhaps, takes to),
You will find over here very good bitter beer, and chops,
      buns, and roast beef, and rump steaks, too!
You can row, fish, or ride, or go bathing beside, in a dress
      rather given to ripping,
Or sit down on the pier, which costs nothing (not dear),
      and talk out, like a tar, on the shipping!
           Though other towns can boast of crowns,
              I think you'll freely own,
            For bathing rare, and breezy air,
              There's nothing like Boulogne!

And although it seems strange, and beyond British range,
      to behold in all decentish weather,
Pretty modest young maids and tall strapping young blades
      side by side in the water together;
Yet we soon get to see, though startling it be, we need find
      no important alarm in it—
For they manage it so that in couples they go, and there's
      sorrow a tittle of harm in it.
Each girl wears a dress that a prude would confess is most
      proper to wear, and each fellow
In a striped trowser-shirt, which fits tight (but don't hurt)
      like a fisher's in MASANIELLO.
They splash and they plunge, and they dive and they lunge,
      and they float and they jump, and they dance, they
      do;
For in all bathing matters they beat us to tatters—They
      manage them better in France, they do!

Boulogne

Though other towns can boast of crowns,
    I think you'll freely own,
For bathing rare, and breezy air,
    There's nothing like Boulogne!

The Etablissement balls, and the dresses and shawls, and
    the brandy—they've always the best of it;
The marvellous dresses, the yellow dyed tresses, vandyked
    petticoats, and the rest of it.
Those old dogs of nineteen, who the world must have seen,
    they so patronize, cherish, and foster us;
Those reckless nerve-shockers, in gay knickerbockers, and
    legs which are simply preposterous.
Then the brave fisher girls, in their earrings and curls, and
    their smiles when you go to buy shrimps of 'em;
And their marvellous legs, like mahogany pegs, and their
    wonderful caps and the crimps of 'em!
And their singular talk as together they walk—never linguist
    attained at the ease of them—
And their jackets in stripes, and their crosses and pipes, and
    their petticoats down to the knees of them!
    Though other towns can boast of crowns,
        I think you'll freely own,
    For bathing rare, and breezy air,
        There's nothing like Boulogne!

MARGATE

EXTENDED on the Margate shore
  (A lazy fit had bound me),
I fell a-moralizing o'er
  The snobs I saw around me.

They buy unholy suits of clothes,
  And every day they don them;
Their speech is crapulous with oaths,
  But still the sun shines on them!

They bawl and holloa, scream and shout,
  Some source of joy they find it—
And though they leave their 'h's out
  The sea don't seem to mind it!

Margate

They spit, and smoke tobacco rank,
   And live incontinently,
And though they look as if they drank,
   The sea air fans them gently!

The words with which themselves they pledge
   Cause decent ears to tingle;
But though it sets one's teeth on edge,
   It don't offend the shingle!

Their showy clothes are slopped with mire,
   Their paws with filth encrusted—
I wonder Nature don't retire
   From public life disgusted.

The sun shines on, the breezes blow,
   When shops and counters free them—
The waves dance gaily to and fro,
   And seem quite glad to see them!

Oh, sun and breeze and dancing trees,
   In one commingling blended,
You are not difficult to please—
   Not easily offended.

THE REVEREND RAWSTON WRIGHT

(Being a Column of Abject Bosh)

Oh! the centre-divided hair,
  And the boots that shine so bright,
And the linen prepared with care,
And the stole and the surplice fair,
  Of the Reverend Rawston Wright.

A popular priest was he,
  And appreciated quite,
And eternally asked to tea
By the whole of his cura*cee*,
  Was the Reverend Rawston Wright.

The Reverend Rawston Wright

The bishop he said, said he,
   "There's no such a shining light
In the whole of my holy see
(Excepting only me),
   As the REVEREND RAWSTON WRIGHT!"

And the vicars they said, said they,
   "Our duty would be but slight
If we could get, some day,
For the moderate sum we pay,
   Such a REVEREND RAWSTON WRIGHT."

But though he was stern all day,
   He'd a singular habit at night—
Indeed, I may fairly say,
An exceedingly singular way
   Had the REVEREND RAWSTON WRIGHT.

He'd strike a gigantic gong,
   And then, the eccentric wight,
Would sing to a wandering throng;
And this was the singular song
   Of the REVEREND RAWSTON WRIGHT:

"Oh, fan an æsthetical flame,
   And sing to the moon so bright,
For piggy-wigs worry and maim,
And my highly respected name
   Is the REVEREND RAWSTON WRIGHT."

And the wondering throng would say,
   "What a strange proceeding quite;

The Reverend Rawston Wright

Will any one tell us, pray,
What means this singular way
  Of the REVEREND RAWSTON WRIGHT? "

But he said, " I find it pays
  To sing it with all my might.
You needn't stand in amaze;
It's only one of the ways
  Of the REVEREND RAWSTON WRIGHT."

And he banged at the gong once more,
  And he danced till the broad daylight,
Then his delicate locks he tore,
And he yelled with a yelping roar,
  Did this singular RAWSTON WRIGHT.

And though he's a serious gent,
  And a popular curate quite,
No man can guess his intent,
Or tell us whatever is meant
  When the REVEREND RAWSTON WRIGHT

Says, " Fan an æsthetical flame,
  And sing to the moon at night,
For piggy-wigs worry and main,
And my highly respected name
  Is the REVEREND RAWSTON WRIGHT! "

A BOULOGNE TABLE-D'HOTE

Air: " He vowed that he never would leave her."

No gathering ever can beat
 Such a treat
 As you meet
 In the people who gather, to eat
At a table-d'hôte every day,
So strange in appearance and phrase
 A leur aise
 In their ways—
As the people who show off their traits
 At a table-d'hôte every day.

A Boulogne Table-d'Hôte

You'll never be tired of meeting
The people who gather for eating
At a table-d'hôte, table-d'hôte, table-d'hôte, table-d'hôte,
    Table-d'hôte every day!

In the Chair an old fellow you'll find—
    He sits there
    In the chair
Because for a fortnight he's dined
    At the table-d'hôte every day.
He's fatherly quite in his ways,
    Looking most
    Like a host,
Your senior by several days.
    He table-d'hôtes every day!
You'll never be tired of meeting
The people who gather for eating
At a table-d'hôte, table-d'hôte, table-d'hôte, table-d'hôte,
    Table-d'hôte every day!

There's another you know at a glance
    Who's designed
    In his mind
To shine in the language of France,
    At the table-d'hôte every day.
" *Hi, Garsong, vous venez ici,*
    Here, I say
    S'il vous plait—
Donnez moi—thanks—all right." He will be
    At the table-d'hôte every day,
You'll never be tired of meeting
The people who gather for eating
At a table-d'hôte, table-d'hôte, table-d'hôte, table-d'hôte,
    Table-d'hôte every day!

A Boulogne Table-d'Hôte

Then the lady so very genteel
That you'd think
She would shrink
From the notion of making a meal
At a table-d'hôte every day.
But you find, though genteel she can eat,
Go right through
The " menoo "
Soup, fish, entrée, joint, cheese, and sweet—
At the table-d'hôte every day.
You'll never be tired of meeting
The people who gather for eating
At a table-d'hôte, table-d'hôte, table-d'hôte, table-d'hôte,
Table-d'hôte every day!

There's the vulgar old glutton and wife,
He who shines
As he dines
And who swallows the blade of his knife
At the table-d'hôte every day,
With his napkin tucked under his chin,
The old bear
Settles there,
Long before it is time to begin,
At the table-d'hôte every day!
You'll never be tired of meeting
The people who gather for eating
At a table-d'hôte, table-d'hôte, table-d'hôte, table-d'hôte,
Table-d'hôte every day!

There's a gay and a gushing old girl,
Who must be
Forty-three
With a seven-and-sixpenny curl,

A Boulogne Table-d'Hôte

At the table-d'hôte every day,
There's also a boy of nineteen
     (Quite a lad)
     Driven mad
By her beauty, who always is seen
At the table-d'hôte every day.
You'll never be tired of meeting
The people who gather for eating
At a table-d'hôte, table-d'hôte, table-d'hôte, table-d'hôte,
Table-d'hôte every day!

PRINCE IL BALEINE

WHEN Autumn boat and train
  Bore London folk to pleasure,
The good PRINCE IL BALEINE
He sought, across the main,
  Amusement for his leisure.

A dusty time, and long,
  He'd had at balls and races,
At crowded levée throng,
At Play and Concert song,
  And various other places.

Prince Il Baleine

But, ah! the British Snob
   Besieged that Prince, in plenty
The Snob adores a Nob,
And follows him, to rob
   His *dolce far niente*!

And finding that the Prince
   Much eagerness to know them
Did not at once evince,
They did not matters mince,
   But begged himself he'd show them.

" Our wishes do not baulk,
   Throw off this English shyness—
And show us how you walk,
And let us hear you talk
   Now do, your Royal Highness!

" You're too reserved, by half:
   Begin perambulating;
We've paid to see you laugh—
We've paid to hear you chaff
   Four gentlemen in waiting.

" Come sit and eat an ice,
   Or drain a bumping measure;
We've practised much device,
And paid a heavy price,
   To see you take your leisure."

[It grieved that PRINCE BALEINE—
   Most sensitive of fishes—

Prince Il Baleine

It always gives him pain
When people can't obtain
   The fulness of their wishes.

But Doctors grave had said,
   " Hang up your stick and beaver;
You *must* have rest and shade,
Or you will soon be laid
   Upon your back with fever."]

No morning when he woke
   But British Snobs addressed him;
His peace of mind they broke,
So up he rose, and spoke
   These words to those who pressed him.

" Oh, over-loyal throng,
   Be guided, pray, by reason:
You may encore a song
(Though that, I think, is wrong),
   But not a London Season!

" I'm told to lie me down
   And rest me at my leisure;
But here's my valet, BROWN,
He's not much worked in town,
   He'll take my place with pleasure!

" I am his special care;
   He brushes, combs, and laves me,
He parts my chestnut hair—
He folds the coats I wear—
   And strops the blade that shaves me.

Prince Il Baleine

" He knows my little ways
  And, though it's not expected,
He'll watch my Royal blaze,
Yet, basking in my rays,
  He'll shine with light reflected."

" Oh, my! " the people cried,
  " To MISTER BROWN I'll bow me!
Oh, ain't he dignified,
Yet not a spark of pride!
  Oh, MISTER BROWN, allow me!

" And so you wash the Prince,
  And pack his clothes for starting,
You scent with jasmine leaf
His pocket-handkerchief,
  And regulate his parting!

" And that, I understand,
  Is your department, is it?
And this then is the hand
That combs at his command?
  Oh, please, do let me kiss it!

" Is this (oh treat of treats!)
  The bedroom that you sleep in?
When cloyed with Royal sweets,
Are these the very sheets
  Which every night you creep in?

" And in this bath you tub,
  Ere out of doors you sally?

Prince Il Baleine

And do these flesh gloves scrub—
These dainty towels rub—
    The Prince's happy *valet*? "

The Snobs, with joy insane,
    Kotoo'd to Brown, unseemly;
And Brown does not complain,
While good Prince il Baleine
    Enjoys his rest extremely.

THE BALLAD OF THE "JIM-JAMS"

WHEN your clothes, from your hat to your socks,
  Have tickled and scrubbed you all day;
When your brain is a musical box
  With a barrel that turns the wrong way;
When you find you're too big for your coat,
  And a great deal too small for your vest,
With a pint of warm oil in your throat,
  And a pound of tin-tacks in your chest;
When you've got a beehive in your head,
  And a sewing machine in each ear;
And you feel that you've eaten your bed,
  And you've got a bad headache down here;
When your lips are like underdone paste,
  And you're highly gamboge in the gill;
And your mouth has a coppery taste,
  As if you'd just bitten a pill;
When everything spins like a top,
  And your stock of endurance gives out;
If some miscreant proposes a chop
  (Mutton-chop, with potatoes and stout),
When your mouth is of flannel—like mine—
  And your teeth not on terms with their stumps,
And spiders crawl over your spine,
  And your muscles have all got the mumps;

The Ballad of the " Jim-Jams "

When you're bad with the creeps and the crawls,
  And the shivers, and shudders, and shakes,
And the pattern that covers the walls
  Is alive with black-beetles and snakes;
When you doubt if your head is your own,
  And you jump when an open door slams,
And you've got to a state which is known
  To the medical world as " jim-jams,"—
    If such symptoms you find
      In your body or head
        They're not easy to quell
    You may make up your mind
      That you're better in bed,
        For you're not at all well!

THE HERMIT

I DON'T suppose you'd ever find
   A man who galloped faster,
To grief of a decisive kind
   Than FREDERIC DISASTER.

I never knew a purer man
   Or one who lived more gently,
But still in every little plan
   He failed incontinently.

For daily bit and daily sup,
   Unfitted quite to battle—
No man has been more shaken up
   In this terrestrial rattle.

The Hermit

Poor FREDERICK succeeded ill
   In every single section,
He could not forge a simple bill
   Or cheque, without detection;

Indeed he often came to grief
   With pots on area railings,
And taking someone's handkerchief
   Ensured immediate jailings.

He couldn't take a pocket-book,
   Or finger people's dials,
But safe detection overtook
   This man of many trials.

I've known him long, and watched his ways
   And seen him growing thinner,
Along of passing many days
   Without a scrap of dinner.

And yet no man more closely bent
   To work than did my neighbour,
For every holiday he spent
   Ensured a year's hard labour.

He worked in Chatham, Devonport,
   And Portland dockyards featly,
I've known him build a bomb-proof fort
   Particularly neatly.

He worked abroad like any horse
   Or other dumb mammalia,
He once passed through a ten years' course
   Road-making in Australia.

The Hermit

But still, though toiling like a brute
   His labour little gained him,
Its anything-but-toothsome fruit
   But scantily sustained him.

But though black-holed he often got,
   And bread-and-watered weekly,
He never murmured at his lot
   But always bore it meekly.

Sometimes he'd say, poor gentle boy,
   " Though lodged and boarded poorly,
E'en such poor boons as I enjoy
   I'm undeserving surely.

" Suppose I quit the world so bright
   And turn a simple hermit—
A dim recluse—an anchorite—
   I don't know what you term it.

" Men, freed from every sinful mesh,
   On herbs and frugal diet,
I'll mortify rebellious flesh
   And live in rural quiet.

" In stony cell without a door
   I'll live and pay no usance
(I've lived in stony cells before
   And found the door a nuisance.)

" In such a cell in mossy glade
   I'll sit, and live austerely;
And sympathetic village maids
   Shall love their hermit dearly.

The Hermit

" The maidens too, before I wake—
  Before I draw my awning,
Shall come and ask me what I'll take
  And how I feel this dawning.

" And every visitor who comes
  To see me in my cavern,
Shall bring me marmalade and plums,
  And dinner from a tavern.

" So, for a skull, a knotted rope,
  And charitable rations,
A robe of sack—a hooded cope,
  And box for small donations,

" I'll freely—willingly resign
  (The pang will not be bitter)
The joys of life which now are mine
  With all their sheen and glitter! "

And so he did! To forest thick
  He fled from worldly folly;
When last I heard from FREDERICK
  He was extremely jolly.

JOPKINS'S GHOST

An Irregular Ballad

Young Jopkins was a waiter,
  A waiter good was he!
One greater—or sedater
  You never sure did see.
He wore a suit of sable—
  From Berlin came his glove;
But he was quite unable
  To overcome his love.

He loved a maid called Betty—
  A pleasing damsel too!
So pretty—but coquette-y!
  He knew not what to do!
But she to be his love
  Declared she would not stoop,
So he dropt a tear—and a Berlin glove—
  In the Mulligatawny soup.

He pined and grew so thin, he
  Was scarce fit for his post;
Like a ninny, he got skinny,
  And as pale as any ghost.

Jopkins's Ghost

His reckoning death was summing,
    And that reckoning was his last;
For though he still said, " Coming,"
    He was going very fast.

Till one day on the table,
    Dead suddenly he drops!
They were able from a label
    To identify his *copse*;
For observing he was growing
    Much too thin for folks to see
He affixed a label, showing—
    (Twasn't grammar)—" This is me! "

But soon there was a talking
    That his ghost was seen at night,
A-walking and a-stalking,
    An attenuated sprite!
But when the cock doth crow,
    It answers, " Coming—coming! "
Adding, " Youths, be warned, and know
    The inconstancy of Wumming! "

INDEX TO FIRST LINES

Index to First Lines

ALPHABETICAL LIST OF TITLES